Rebekah and I have been friends for a long time. We've celebrated plenty of good times, and she has seen me through some hard times. One thing has remained consistent: she's never told me what to do; she's reminded me of *who I am*. She's helped me refocus. This is what Rebekah has done once again in this book. She's brought a boat load of transparency and authenticity to these pages with the hope that you'll stop letting what's distracting you keep you from your much greater purposes. You're going to connect with what she has to say.

BOB GOFF, author of *Love Does* and *Everybody Always*

Time spent caring for your emotional, physical, relational, and spiritual health is never wasted. It is a necessary and God-honoring practice—one we would do well to stop and consider. I'm thankful for friends like Rebekah who remind us that in order to pursue God's highest and best, we must first seek his ways of renewal, where weary souls find wisdom, renewal, and peace.

LYSA TERKEURST, #1 *New York Times* bestselling author and president of Proverbs 31 Ministries

In *Rhythms of Renewal*, my close friend and mentor Rebekah Lyons leads readers on an inspiring, insightful, practical journey to life-giving peace and purpose. *Rhythms of Renewal* is timely and much needed for my generation. It's a joy to recommend this book to everyone!

SADIE ROBERTSON, author, speaker, and founder of Live Original

A great number of us suffer from some aspect of anxiety or stress. These issues can rob our joy, disturb our relationships, and paralyze our dreams. Rebekah Lyons has created an approach to dealing well with these. If you or someone you know struggles with anxiety and stress, you will find answers and hope that make sense and work. Highly recommended.

JOHN TOWNSEND, Ph.D., *New York Times* bestselling author of *Boundaries* and *People Fuel*, and founder of the Townsend Institute for Leadership and Counseling

I love how faith and a life of emotional wellness are so connected. Rebekah Lyons brings us the best of both in *Rhythms of Renewal* and offers practical, daily rhythms on how to live free.

CANDACE CAMERON BURE, actress and author

We humans have short memories. In our haste, we forget that we have been created as rhythmic beings, reflecting our deep connection to the entire creation. We need to be reminded, and Rebekah Lyons has done just that. With *Rhythms of Renewal*, she draws our attention with kindness and clarity to those actions whose engagement will create the space and embodied encounters that Jesus so longs to use for his generative purposes in our lives. Read this book and learn to flourish in the cadence of our God.

CURT THOMPSON, MD, psychiatrist, speaker, and author of *The Soul of Shame* and *Anatomy of the Soul*

Looking back on a personal season wherein I failed to give myself the permission to rest in order to thrive, I cannot exclaim loudly enough the value in the dynamic design of REST and the rhythms that my trusted friend Rebekah shares with us in this book, providing a sanctuary space to restore and revitalize the passions and gifts that God has given us to use for his glory.

ELISABETH HASSELBECK, author of *Point of View: A Fresh Look at Work, Faith, and Freedom*

As a high schooler, I see the impact anxiety, depression, and stress are having on my friends and community. I love how Rebekah Lyons draws from her own battles and then encourages us to fight daily for rhythms of joy and rest. This is a must-read for all, especially high school girls!

ALENA PITTS, singer, actress, author

Rebekah Lyons has given us a great gift. Rarely does a book combine a compelling vision, theological insights, and a vision of practical faith so well. This book touches a deep longing we all have for a more beautiful and sustainable life, one lived to the depth and height of what God actually offers. You will find rest for your soul and strength for your heart in here.

JON TYSON, Church of the City New
York, author of *The Burden is Light*

Many of us race through life without dealing with the stress and anxiety restlessness causes. In *Rhythms of Renewal*, Rebekah explores the practices that renew and refresh our souls. Read and reclaim the life God has for you!

LISA BEVERE, *New York Times* bestselling author
and cofounder of Messenger International

I remember being in a small gathering of leaders the first time I heard Rebekah talk about the rhythms of renewal. She hadn't written a book yet; it was simply what God was teaching her. I was taking notes as fast as I could, and I was deeply impacted by what she shared that day. The message of rhythm was one that was all at once inspiring, convicting, challenging, and accessible. *Rhythms of Renewal* is a message that we must hear and embrace more than ever before.

BANNING LIEBSCHER, pastor, founder
of Jesus Culture, and author of *Rooted: The
Hidden Places Where God Develops You*

RHYTHMS of RENEWAL

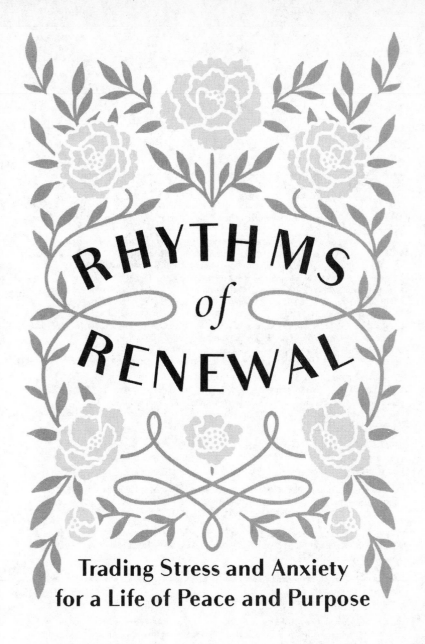

RHYTHMS
of
RENEWAL

**Trading Stress and Anxiety
for a Life of Peace and Purpose**

REBEKAH LYONS

ZONDERVAN®

ZONDERVAN

Rhythms of Renewal
Copyright © 2019 by Rebekah Lyons

Requests for information should be addressed to:
Zondervan, *3900 Sparks Dr. SE, Grand Rapids, Michigan 49546*

ISBN 978-0-310-35617-2 (international trade paper edition)

ISBN 978-0-310-35619-6 (audio)

Library of Congress Cataloging-in-Publication Data

Names: Lyons, Rebekah, author.
Title: Rhythms of renewal : trading stress and anxiety for a life of peace and purpose / Rebekah Lyons.
Description: Grand Rapids : Zondervan, 2019. | Includes bibliographical references. | Summary:
  "Daily struggles with anxiety and stress make it difficult to receive God's peace. In Rhythms
  of Renewal, Rebekah Lyons helps you walk through four rhythms to the vibrant life you were
  meant to live. By learning to rest, renew, connect, and create, you will find mindful habits that
  quiet inner chaos and make space for the peace you long for"— Provided by publisher.
Identifiers: LCCN 2019026018 (print) | LCCN 2019026019 (ebook) | ISBN 9780310356141
  (hardcover) | ISBN 9780310356189 (epub)
Subjects: LCSH: Anxiety—Religious aspects—Christianity. | Christian life.
Classification: LCC BV4908.5 .L965 2019 (print) | LCC BV4908.5 (ebook) | DDC 248.8/6—dc23
LC record available at https://lccn.loc.gov/2019026018
LC ebook record available at https://lccn.loc.gov/2019026019

Cover illustration: Dana Tanamachi
Interior design: Aaron Campbell and Denise Froehlich

Printed in the United States of America

19 20 21 22 23 LSC 10 9 8 7 6 5 4

FOR GABE, MY HUSBAND OF
TWENTY-TWO YEARS.

YOU HELPED ME LIVE INTO THESE RHYTHMS
AND CHAMPIONED THESE WORDS FROM
THE BEGINNING. ALL MY LOVE.

CONTENTS

CONNECT RHYTHM

CREATE RHYTHM

WHEN THE DOORS WON'T OPEN

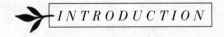

INTRODUCTION

WHEN THE DOORS WON'T OPEN

———

O n a brisk Saturday afternoon in October, the panic returned. I was nestled high above California's northern coast, near the sleepy town of Carmel, attending a gathering of mostly young couples, old friends, and a few new acquaintances. We'd met for a much-needed retreat, time away to refocus our hearts and minds for the season ahead. That afternoon, the group made a collective decision. We'd disband for a little free time, tour the quaint village of Carmel-by-the Sea, and enjoy a latte, pastry, or gelato. We could take it easy. Relax.

We were staying at no ordinary home. This was architect Charles S. Greene's one-hundred-year-old magnum opus. He called it Seaward, meaning "toward the sea," a name which captures the scene well. A library lined with antique classics and a Palladian window overlooked the rocky beach. I needed a moment in front of that window, a pause before rejoining the group for the midday caffeine and sugar boost. I told my husband, Gabe, to go on ahead with our friends, and I'd catch up thirty minutes later, after some reflection in that beautiful setting.

Not five minutes after my friends left, I headed to the bathroom. Like every other part of the structure, even the tiny toilet area seemed hand-carved out of stone. It was a tight space. Confined.

But I didn't think twice about it as I entered and latched the door behind me.

Glancing at my phone, I watched as it lost power too fast, shutting off yet again at 45 percent. *Crazy old iPhone.* I'd been reluctant to upgrade because of the expense, but I could no longer ignore that it was losing over 50 percent of the battery power in only an hour. I made a mental note to upgrade when the trip was over, stood, flushed, and turned the century-old lock and door handle. The latch didn't give. I turned again and again and again, then, using both hands, turned with everything I had. Nothing. I toggled the handle back and forth. I waited for the click of the internal mechanism releasing, but it never came.

A one-hundred-year-old home on the cliffs of the Pacific. Locked in a two-foot-by-four-foot space. Cement walls ten inches thick all around. Heavy, wooden, one-hundred-year-old door. Alone for the next few hours. Cell phone dead.

The walls began to close in, squeezing the breath from me. Within fifteen seconds, my body was convulsing. I was trapped. No one to call. No place to turn. Except in tiny circles.

Rational or not, I couldn't wrap my mind around the idea of sitting in that two-by-four-foot cement stall until someone returned hours later to my knocking and crying. And that's when the questions came.

Why was this so terrifying?

Wasn't I supposed to be better?

Hadn't I recovered from these panic attacks years ago?

I guess relapse has a way of finding each of us.

All my life I'd been resilient, working my way around obstacles. No finances to finish college? I worked two jobs to cover tuition and rent. Not enough money for a car? I hustled to earn credit to qualify for a lease. No slush fund to pay for a wedding? I emptied two years of savings into a tight budget, starting with a $300 wedding dress. No matter what doors slammed in life, I rebounded with ways to shove them open. There was no obstacle that couldn't be overcome with grit and a dash of elbow grease.

————

A ONE-HUNDRED-YEAR-OLD HOME ON THE CLIFFS OF THE PACIFIC. LOCKED IN A TWO-FOOT-BY-FOUR-FOOT SPACE. CEMENT WALLS TEN INCHES THICK ALL AROUND. HEAVY, WOODEN, ONE-HUNDRED-YEAR-OLD DOOR. ALONE FOR THE NEXT FEW HOURS. CELL PHONE DEAD.

————

But here was one door I couldn't open. No amount of working or achievement or self-talk could break me out of this bathroom prison high above the sea. I was left with myself, my frailty, my inability to escape, and it terrified me. And the truth was, I wasn't terrified of the heavy wooden door or the unyielding antique lock. I was terrified of being trapped, terrified of being alone and witnessing my body's outrage. I was terrified of *me*.

What could I do under this duress? Even though I wasn't in harm's way, it mattered not, because the greatest perpetrator of harm was tucked inside my mind. I worked the loops of panic and terror over and over, searching for any way of escape.

Then I looked up.

At the top of the wall, I noticed a small arched window, approximately twenty inches tall and eighteen inches wide. I toggled the antique latch, and to my surprise, it opened. I squealed in overwhelming disbelief, and tears erupted. *Could it be?* If I hoisted myself up on the tank of the toilet, I could jimmy my body through the window head-first. Would my hips fit? It didn't matter. Rescue was in sight, and I was going for it.

Once my body was out to my waist, I inhaled deeply, filling my lungs with cold, salty air. I heard the seagulls squawking, the ocean waves pounding, nature doing what it does while my life seemed to be spiraling out of control. I kept pushing, kept shoving my hips and legs until I toppled onto the rocks overlooking the waves crashing below. I thought my thigh muscles would never stop convulsing. Crouching there in a fetal position, I wept. Everything I had faced six years prior—the panic attacks, the unbearable anxiety, the meltdowns—came flooding back, along with all the shame and weakness.

I'd struggled with panic attacks daily in the year after our family moved to Manhattan, mostly when I found myself in confined spaces like planes, trains, or shoulder-to-shoulder crowds. Elevators were the worst. At Bloomingdale's, I stood at the first-floor bank of elevators for twenty minutes and watched, waiting for the perfect conditions to hop on—at least two other people on the elevator but no more than five. Once those conditions were finally met, I walked in, and as the doors clamped shut, my heart froze. I stood, holding my breath, fists clenched, until the doors opened at the ninth floor. No matter how many times I made that trip, the panic was always the same.

On the night of September 20, 2011, I cried out to God for relief, and he flooded me with peace. In the years following, I traveled and spoke about freedom from panic, and I'd even written *You Are Free*, a book about finding freedom from anxiety. Why had it returned now, seven years later?

I asked God, "Am I a fraud?" How was it that I could speak to so many people about being healed of panic disorder, write a book about it, pray for others to find healing, and find myself facing a panic attack more severe than any attack I'd experienced in Bloomingdale's? I stared blankly across the ocean, let the wind whip against my tear-stained cheeks, the questions ringing in my ears. I knew God saw me with compassion and tenderness, but he wasn't responding to my questions. Not yet.

As my heartbeat slowed to its resting rate, I rallied and went to meet up with my friends. I could hear the rest of the group laughing down the block. They were swept up in conversation, so I slipped in with a nod. I listened with a pasted-on smile, a thousand miles away from whatever they were saying. The rest of the day was a blur. I kept slipping away to look out across the Pacific, mysterious and vast, as if God would use his handiwork to give me an answer to all these new questions.

That night, before going to sleep, I tried to explain to Gabe what had happened, but no words seemed to give the right amount of weight to the trauma of that afternoon. As he rolled over in bed, and his steady breathing slowed, I stared at the ceiling in the dark. Tears flowed from the corners of my eyes, pooling in my ears. I asked again with a whisper, *How can it be? Seven years of teaching, healing, and freedom?* Had the truth been stolen in a single incident? Why were shame and loneliness setting in?

In his mercy, God gently whispered a response: *You can focus on the fact that fear came knocking, or you can focus on the fact that I always make a way of escape.*

There it was, the love of God, and it sounded like the Scripture I'd committed to memory years ago: "I will always make a way of escape . . . that you will be able to bear it."[1]

YOU CAN FOCUS ON THE FACT THAT FEAR CAME KNOCKING, OR YOU CAN FOCUS ON THE FACT THAT I ALWAYS MAKE A WAY OF ESCAPE.

DO YOU NEED RESCUE?

Have you found yourself trapped in fear? Feelings of unworthiness? Rejection? Loneliness? Depression? Isolation? Restlessness or boredom? If so, know this: God makes a way of escape. Not only that, but he promises a life of abundance—a rich life—not just escape from negative cycles.

Rescue is ready and waiting for us, but so often, we are unable to see a way of escape. Instead of looking up, we keep our heads down, circling the stall, wondering why our circumstances don't change. We get lost in our loops, repeat the same habits over and over, expecting different results. Insane? I'd say so.

What do you do when stress or anxiety or fatigue or discouragement hits, when it throbs in your ribs or steals your breath? When your words race and you try a desperate attempt to yawn and fill your lungs? What do you do when this is the norm of your everyday life?

What do you do when relapse hits? When silence settles, distraction fades, and you face panic, depression, or burnout again? What do you do when you descend into anxiety after being panic-free for years, after walking in a place of freedom or abundance?

These are the questions many of us are asking today. According to the American Institute of Stress (AIS), 77 percent of the population experiences physical symptoms associated with stress on a regular basis, 33 percent report living with extreme stress, and 48 percent say stress has a negative impact on their personal and professional lives.[2] The AIS estimates the aggregate cost to employers of stress-related healthcare expenses and missed work is $300 billion annually.[3] What's more, according to the National Alliance on Mental Illness (NAMI), 18 percent of American adults currently suffer from an anxiety disorder, and some estimate close to 35 percent of the population experience anxiety disorders.[4] The NAMI also indicates nearly 7 percent of the population struggles with depression.[5]

As a society, we are in the throes of a collective panic attack. We pursue anxiety-inducing careers, security, and keeping up. We're afraid we're not doing enough. We worry about health, or politics, or other things we can't control. That's when discouragement settles in. Mental and emotional fatigue takes over. Fear and anxiety overcome. Finally, despair prevails.

As long as there is darkness in this world, we'll be tempted to disengage or give in to anxiety and fear. But over and over, Scripture tells us not to fear. As Jesus said, "I am leaving you with a gift—peace of mind and heart. And the peace I give is a gift the world cannot give. So don't be troubled or afraid."[6]

The command not to fear is given over three hundred times (some say 365 times, once for every day of the year). In fact, it's a phrase used more than any other command in the Bible,[7] because God knew that as long as fear lives in our hearts, we'd live crippled lives. We would shortchange the plans and purposes destined for us from the womb.

If there's one thing I've learned in seven years on this road, a lesson that's been confirmed by person after person I've spoken with, it's this: with a little intention and a lot of perseverance, stress and anxiety can be transformed into peace and purpose. Boredom and depression can become excitement and engagement.

What kind of intention?

That's what this book is all about.

RHYTHMS THAT BRING RENEWAL

Through study and experience, I've come to understand four rhythms that help us replace stress and anxiety with life-giving peace and purpose. They help us nurture and sustain lasting emotional health. These rhythms aren't complicated—Rest, Restore, Connect, and Create—and they're words I first wrote under the heading "Rhythms of Renewal" the summer I found my own freedom. However, these rhythms do take practice. Practical acts like fasting from media (Rest), exercising (Restore), sharing a laugh (Connect), or recovering an old talent (Create) can help us break the anxiety-inducing cycles of the world around us and bring balance to our otherwise hectic lives. They can help us cultivate the spiritual and mental space needed to allow God to bring us through complacency and fear and into freedom.

When you consider it, these four rhythms make some sense. The first two—Rest and Restore—are "input rhythms," rhythms that allow the peace of Jesus to fill us. The latter two rhythms—Connect and Create—are "output rhythms," rhythms that pull us out of our own heads and help us engage with the world around us. It's the input of Christ's peace that allowed me to pour out that peace, and when I abide in that input-and-output flow, I don't struggle so much with anxiety. In fact, I find healing and wholeness. (A word of caution: the practices contained in this book aren't meant to replace professional treatment for those who need it. That said, they can be used in conjunction with therapy to bring renewal and peace.)

My hope is that that ten years from now, you'll look back on your own season of stress or defeat and see how God brought you back to center through the rhythms of renewal outlined in this book. My prayer is that you'll see how these spiritual rhythms enabled you to live a life of peace, passion, and purpose.

REST

I've never been great at Rest. I'm as overworked, overstimulated, and overextended as the next person. There are demands on my life, and it can be hard to slow down. This nonstop pace leads to more stress and more anxiety. If I've discovered anything over the years, it's this: my anxiety spins back up when I'm not resting.

We are restless when we rest less.

We weren't created for this nonstop pace. We were designed in God's image, and even God himself rested. As recorded in Genesis, after creating the world, God set aside the seventh day to rest. In Genesis 2 the Bible states, "on the seventh day he rested from all his work. Then God blessed the seventh day and made it holy, because on it he rested from all the work of creating that he had done."[1]

Rest precedes blessing. We don't have to run to *earn* rest; we run *fueled by* a posture of rest.

God also calls the day he rested *holy*. He saw rest as sacred, and later decreed his people to observe the Sabbath and have reverence for a defined, consistent pattern of rest. He promised peace to those who rest: "'I will grant peace in the land, and you will lie down and no one will make you afraid."[2] This followed the promise, "If you follow my decrees and are careful to obey my commands, I will send you rain in its season, and the ground will yield its crops and the trees their fruit."[3] And finally, he says in verse nine, "I will look on you with favor and make you fruitful."[4]

WE DON'T HAVE TO RUN TO *EARN* REST; WE
RUN *FUELED BY* A POSTURE OF REST.

God meant for all our work to culminate in holy, blessed rest—rest meant to help us reconnect with him. He intended for us to live fruitful lives, to have hearts full of peace.

We live in a society that is over-stressed, over-anxious, and burned out. What's the remedy? Rest. God-blessed rest. In this section, I will introduce rhythmic practices that can help us find the rest we need, rest that will protect and rejuvenate us. You might find that some of these ways of rest come more easily than others. In fact, you might already be soaking in Scripture and reflection (both forms of rest). Likewise, you might find that some practices—like engaging in a technology detox or taking a Sabbath day—seem nearly impossible. But as you read, take note of the various ways you can practice the rhythm of rest. Ask yourself which practices you might need most, and set aside time for them. And remember, if you're not a natural rest-er, this might take a little time. That's okay. Be patient with yourself.

Are you ready to bring rest to your restlessness? Let's learn how.

TAKE INVENTORY

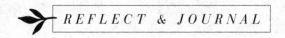

REFLECT & JOURNAL

CHAPTER 1

TAKE INVENTORY

REFLECT & JOURNAL

The unexamined life is not worth living.

—SOCRATES

P arker Palmer's book *Let Your Life Speak* arrested my heart a few years back. It begins with a poem by William Stafford, "Ask Me", that begs this question: "Some time when the river is ice ask me mistakes I have made. Ask me whether what I have done is my life.[1] It was the first book that challenged me to take inventory of my days, to consider my thoughts, actions, and daily routine. I began to ask myself, *Is the life I lead the life that longs to live in me?*

When I first asked myself this question, my life was consumed with Target returns and Chick-fil-A playdates. It had been a decade swallowed by Pull-Ups and pacifiers and poop. Though these motherhood moments weren't the whole of my life's longing, they were largely the makeup of my days. I'd never considered the life that longed to live in me.

Fast-forward eighteen years. I'm not only organizing playdates, I'm navigating first dates. We've moved from Pull-Ups to outfitting our kids in sports jerseys and athletic gear for summer camp. Raising four children, three of whom are now teenagers, comes with a boatload of bustle. But no matter the season—whether new motherhood or raising teens—pausing to take inventory has saved my life. When I find myself too busy for it, I'm lost. When I make time for it, I gain critical perspective.

WHAT IS TAKING INVENTORY?

What does it mean to take inventory? I'm not talking about cleaning out cabinets, counting pairs of shoes, or hunting down missing Christmas decorations. (We'll get to that later.) I'm describing the important practice of evaluating my life and redefining priorities to ensure I'm living it well.

Several years ago, I realized something significant was missing in my life. I sensed my purpose was to extend beyond homemaking, that my work was meant to be both inside and outside our home. There was only one problem: our existing schedule had no margin for me to imagine what my role outside the home might be. There were subtle glimpses of a writing gift, and I caught them each time I snuck downstairs in the middle of the night to download the burdens of my heart on my laptop. Writing was the only way I knew to process what God might be doing in my life. What did that mean?

Together, my husband, Gabe, and I decided to sort it all out. We started by creating space to take inventory, carved out time from our busy schedules to dream. We began writing down all the moments when I felt most alive. We talked about my love for reading, writing, and communication, and started connecting the dots. Then we noted the moments where I felt at my worst, those moments when I couldn't get a break from the endless responsibilities of raising children. I felt there wasn't enough time to express the gifts God had given me. As we took inventory of those moments, God's vision for my life came into focus.

What if my gift and knack for the written and spoken word could be used for something bigger than myself? Maybe I could take a year to explore this more and live into a different reality. We started dreaming about how God might use the tensions I was facing as I tried to live the life that longed to live in me.

Looking back, I can see how taking a break, resting from responsibility long enough to take inventory, was crucial to imagining God's plan for my life. With Gabe's help and support, I learned how to establish rhythms for writing and teaching, fulfilling work I couldn't imagine before we began to take inventory. I'm grateful to see the fruit of those rhythms not just for myself, but also for others. Women inspire me every day as they press into their greater purposes from a place of emotional, spiritual, and mental health. Most importantly, God's kindness blows me away. He invites scores of people to gain a deeper understanding of the freedom they can experience in Christ as they live out their callings and use their gifts.

HOW TO TAKE INVENTORY

Much of our anxiety and depression stems from uncertainty about the future. We toss and turn, obsess and review, in the hope that we can find the magic pill, the answer to our uncertainty. But if you take away anything from this book, you'll find there is no one thing that solves everything. It's a combination of habits, patterns, and rhythms that keeps the angst at bay. You'll never discover these principles if you don't pause to take inventory, and although resting from the day's work long enough to do so may seem counterproductive, it might be the most beneficial thing you do.

So how do you take inventory? Consider starting small.

Every day I ask myself questions such as, *Where is God leading me? What new people has he placed in my path? What new commitment is he asking me to make?* I try to act on the obvious and immediate, and to note any big revelations I may need to come back to when I have extended time.

WHERE IS GOD LEADING ME?
WHAT NEW PEOPLE HAS HE PLACED IN MY PATH?
WHAT NEW COMMITMENT IS HE ASKING ME TO MAKE?

I also set aside a few hours quarterly and take a deeper dive. I start by acknowledging all the pushes and pulls on my life. Using a rubric that helps keep it simple, I ask four simple questions I learned from our mentor, Pete Richardson, and make a simple list to get my head in the right direction.

The first question, **What's Right?** keeps me aware of and grateful for the gifts in my life. Grounding ourselves in recognition of the good sets a positive tone for the rest of the inventory.

Asking **What's Wrong?** allows me to see where things have veered off course. By answering this question, I assess and name the challenges I'm facing. I take time to name those things that feel off or out of order. In naming what's wrong, I take the first step in solving my problems.

The third question, **What's Confused?** helps me isolate the rabbit trails I seem to chase to no end. Am I teaching our children respect and responsibility? Am I making friendships a priority? Is our time together as a family quality time? I could spend an endless amount of mental energy considering these questions over the course of my day, but when I carve out time to process it on the page, the answers become clear. Writing it down, I find the anxiety associated with these questions dissipates.

The last question, **What's Missing?** requires a hard look at areas of life I may be too close to, areas I can't evaluate alone. To answer this question, I need help and insight from Gabe and a few trusted friends. This community question helps me identify blind spots or talk through my desires to ensure they are rooted in the story God has called me to live.

Reflecting for a few moments every day and doing a deeper dive every few months keeps us aware of the anxiety-producing things in our lives and allows us to correct course. If you find the process as beneficial as I have, you may find a deeper, multiple-day annual Personal Inventory Retreat offers even more clarity, because it creates additional space for new dreams to emerge. You'll be surprised how suppressed passions surface, how solutions to your problems emerge when you take time away.

THEME YOUR INVENTORY

Sometimes I choose a theme for my examinations. Last year, for example, I chose the theme "Re-establish." I felt an urgency to re-examine and better integrate the responsibilities of motherhood and career. For fifteen years, I'd known only the former, but in the last five years, I'd been pushing into the latter. I felt like things were out of balance, like it was one or the other, and I didn't want to reside on the extremes of the pendulum anymore. The extremes left me frazzled or grabbing for control. I needed to re-establish who I was both as a mother *and* as a career woman. So I challenged myself to embrace the imperfections of carrying both. With this theme in mind, I took inventory again. I realized that I didn't need to answer every email on the same day. Nor did I need to wash every dirty dish the same day. But I would always leave room for an extra bedtime story.

It's never too late to re-establish what you want your life to be about.

If we do our inventories right, it will be a holy process. A day is coming when each of us will give an account of how we stewarded our time, our years, and the beloved people entrusted to our care.[2] When we rest long enough to take inventory, when we ask God to cultivate our heart, talents, and passions according to the purpose he planned before our days began,[3] we'll find new horizons opening up, horizons beyond all we could ask or imagine.[4]

———

IT'S NEVER TOO LATE TO RE-ESTABLISH WHAT
YOU WANT YOUR LIFE TO BE ABOUT.

———

It's easy to get caught up in the endless, anxiety-inducing cycles of producing or parenting or networking or serving. It's easy to believe we can't rest from our work, that we have to push, push, push into the next obligation or we'll fall behind. But we have to rest from those cycles long enough to take inventory. If we don't, we might miss God's best for us, the plan that will bring us ultimate rest from a very demanding world.

⏹ REFLECTION QUESTIONS ⏹

1. DESCRIBE YOUR LIFE. WHAT IS WRONG, MISSING, OR CONFUSING IN YOUR LIFE?

2. HOW LONG HAS IT BEEN SINCE YOU'VE TAKEN INVENTORY OF YOUR LIFE? HAVE YOU EVER?

3. WRITE OUT A PLAN FOR HOW YOU CAN STEP AWAY, EVEN FOR HALF A DAY, AND TAKE INVENTORY.

TECH
DETOX

SILENCE THE NOISE

CHAPTER 2

TECH DETOX

SILENCE THE NOISE

*We are continually being nudged by our devices
toward a set of choices. The question is whether those
choices are leading us to the life we actually want.*

—ANDY CROUCH

It's been eight years since I started using Instagram. May 7, 2011, to be exact. We'd moved to the Upper East Side of New York City the previous summer, and though many of my friends were becoming more active on social networking platforms, I was not a savvy social-media user. I hadn't embraced Facebook or Twitter, but the idea of keeping a real-time photo journal to share with friends and family? This was something I could get behind. After one weekend of using the photo-sharing app, I was hooked.

New York was eye candy to me in those days. My first post was of the hot dog cart on our street corner (61st Street and 3rd Avenue) on my morning walk to Central Park, the same cart that would rattle over the same pothole each and every day at five a.m. When I look at the photo today, I can still hear that cart, as clear as I could from my bed on the fourth floor of our apartment building.

Day after day, I captured pictures of the park: our walk home from school, nights out riding city streets on the Vespa with Gabe. I captured silly moments with the kids in our big-city playground, documented our season of awe and wonder with a child's perspective. I wanted to keep an account for my own memory bank, a record of this life-transforming season.

For three years I kept sharing moments; there was never a shortage of sights to capture through the lens. I added captions, thoughtful anecdotes that surfaced each day from the pages of my journal. What began as memory-making became something more as I began to search for the perfect angle, lighting, and story. As the number of my followers grew, so did the compulsion to share. I became more strategic, gave people what I thought they wanted, fearing they'd leave if I didn't. Anything less seemed self-indulgent, at least that's what I told myself. In that season, without me realizing it, social media became the master. I became the slave.

Instead of taking time to process the moments of my life, instead of reflecting in solitude over weeks, months, even, I processed everything in real time in the company of strangers. Whenever I felt anxiety setting in, I'd grab my phone, the distraction of choice. I filled my mind with everyone else's noise, no matter how much it might cost.

Gabe noticed before I did. "You don't need to capture *everything*; just enjoy the moment!" he said. Kennedy, my daughter, saw it too, and would ask, "Can you stop looking at your phone?" While it was fun to document special experiences, my family didn't sign up for our lives to be on display for public entertainment.

It would take seven years for the reality of this to set in. In the spring of 2018, I felt God whispering that I should fast from social media. I dismissed and defended my actions. *It's no big deal, God. It doesn't mean that much to me.*

I woke up a few weeks later feeling an urge, a conviction even, to press pause for a season. I couldn't wait another day. So I shared online that I needed to take a hiatus from social media, a break for me, for my family. I wanted to consider the consequences of living an over-shared life. It wasn't a hand slap, but an invitation. An invitation to what? I wasn't sure, but I'd soon find out.

THE EFFECTS OF A SOCIAL MEDIA FAST

When I jumped off social media, things changed. First, I started dreaming again. On the back porch, journal in hand, new ideas and thoughts flooded my mind. I wasn't copying, comparing, or envying the lives of others. Something shifted deep in my spirit. Unconcerned about what others might think, I logged reflections, took note of new dreams that began to emerge.

Second, I was sleeping better than ever. My full night's sleep routine kicked back in almost immediately. After years of early morning wake-ups and feelings of insomnia, my mind and body were catching up on much-needed rest. I stopped scrolling through my social media apps before bed, so my body and brain were better prepared for sleep. If I woke for a moment in the middle of the night, I refrained from checking my phone, knowing it might keep me awake.

Third, I pursued learning again. Every choice to peruse social media was a choice *not* to do something productive with my time, and in that extra time garnered by fasting from it, I read more books, listened to more podcasts and talks. In the first two months of my Instagram fast, I digested more centering content than I'd listened to in the previous *year*. My mind felt renewed as my passion for learning returned. Years of consuming the media, opinions, and experiences of others had created a deficit. Now, without all those inputs, my brain was hungry for growth.

A month into this experiment, this rest from social media, I was driving home at sunset through the rolling hills of Franklin, Tennessee, where we had moved from New York. I passed around a bend in the road and gasped at the sky, ablaze with pinks and reds. My eyes welled up at the beauty. Normally, I would have pulled over to the side of the road and angle for the perfect shot to share on Instagram. Even before I reached for my phone, I realized I didn't have it with me—and I didn't care. I drove on, reflecting on this change of heart, mind, and soul for a few more minutes. That's when God reminded me of the truth I needed to hear: *You are worthy to receive something beautiful, and you don't have to share it.*

YOU ARE WORTHY TO RECEIVE SOMETHING
BEAUTIFUL, AND YOU DON'T HAVE TO SHARE IT.

That's when I pulled over to the side of that country road. I stared across the amber sky and started to ponder, *Why do I feel so compelled to share everything? Whose validation am I seeking?* Somewhere along the way, I'd decided that anything I did just for me felt indulgent, and I didn't believe I was worthy of indulgence. What began as a break from the constant churn of social media became a fundamental lesson in worthiness. I came to see that my worth is not found in approval "out there." It is found in the loving gifts God offers in the "right now," in the intimate invitation of a sunset.

Far too many of us race through life full-throttle from photo to photo, achievement to achievement. We jump from distraction to distraction, image to image, issue to issue, never stopping to ask *why*. No wonder we are anxious and stressed!

Resting from technology, from social media or the internet or our smart phones, slows us down, makes space for us to examine our blind spots, and gives us greater capacity to be present to the moment right in front of us. At least, it did for me.

REENTRY IS POSSIBLE

I reentered social media a couple months later, cautious about beginning again. Soon after, I shared with a friend how grateful I was for a slower pace, longer attention span, and my diminishing need for public approval. I shared how I could read an entire book again without being sidetracked and engage in a long conversation without reaching for my phone. I told her how I see the flicker in my Kennedy's eyes when she's excited to share something from her day, and I give her my whole attention. How I catch our son Cade's goofy smirk when he's up to no good; how I'm present enough to laugh. By resting from social media, I'd recovered the lost art of *paying attention*, and somehow, that brought me a sense of peace and tranquility.

Through this refreshing season of dreaming, sleeping, and learning, I'd also found my true voice again. I wanted to encourage people online from an overflow, not post out of pressure to keep up, like the old days. Something clicked as I reflected, saying to myself, *If you lose your voice, be quiet a while. It'll come back.*

My friend listened, and when I was finished sharing, she was smiling. She wanted that too, she said. Don't you?

If you find yourself anxiously comparing, constantly distracted, eternally envious of what others share on social media or the internet, consider the words of Paul to the church in Galatians: "For am I now seeking the approval of man, or of God? Or am I trying to please man? If I were still trying to please man, I would not be a servant of Christ."[1] What better way to practice this teaching than by taking a tech detox.

Maybe you should fast from Instagram, or Twitter, or Facebook. Maybe you should leave your smart phone in a box by the front door when you walk in after a long day. Consider limiting the number of texts you send in a day. Try it out and give yourself the rest your mind, soul, and body need—for your sake and for the sake of those around you.

⤳ REFLECTION QUESTIONS ⤦

1. HOW MUCH SOCIAL MEDIA DO YOU CONSUME IN A WEEK? DO YOU HAVE A SCREEN TIME TRACKER THAT RECORDS YOUR TIME? (THERE ARE A FEW GOOD ONES OUT THERE, INCLUDING THE TRACKERS BUILT INTO YOUR PHONE.)

2. TAKE A BREAK FROM ALL SOCIAL MEDIA FOR TWO WEEKS. AT THE END OF THAT TWO WEEKS, ASK YOURSELF: WHAT DO I MISS ABOUT IT? WHAT DON'T I MISS? WRITE OUT YOUR ANSWERS.

3. WHAT POSITIVES DO YOU ASSIGN TO THE USE OF TECHNOLOGY IN YOUR LIFE? WHAT NEGATIVES?

GET QUIET

CREATE SPACE AND LISTEN

CHAPTER 3

CHAPTER 3

GET QUIET

CREATE SPACE AND LISTEN

Without great solitude, no serious work is possible.

—PABLO PICASSO

G rowing up, I always considered myself an extrovert. I never declined an invitation or opportunity to hang with friends. If homework or studying for a test threatened to get in the way, I'd pull an all-nighter. College life suited me. There were late night hangs in the dorm, morning workouts with friends, and I made sure my friends and I had plans after each Saturday football game. I was enthusiastic about life, and *the more the merrier* was my modus operandi.

After graduation, things began to change. When I became a mom of toddlers, I craved alone time. Closing the door to the bathroom felt sacred. When those toddlers grew up and became teens, I'd linger in the car in the garage for a few moments after they went inside. This shift in me showed up in other ways as well. Instead of exercising in a noisy, crowded gym, I began to prefer morning workouts involving yoga and nature hikes. To make room for a longer pause of quiet at home, I set aside two days a week for running errands and meeting friends for lunch or coffee. On the mornings I wasn't running around, I spent large swaths of time at home, sitting in the quiet.

I've flown a lot over the last five years, and on one flight, it hit me: The reason I enjoyed flying was that it offered me quiet and a chance to recharge. During a flight I could catch up on podcasts and talks; I could journal, read, and prep for what I would be speaking about later that night. When I arrived at the event, I was energized and ready to engage at full capacity for a long evening until everyone went home. I loved both the intense connection with people for long periods of time and the retreat to a silent hotel room.

What did that mean? Was I becoming an introvert?

Discovering just how much I loved less noisy spaces, I picked up Susan Cain's book *Quiet,* in which she writes, "Introverts . . . may have strong social skills and enjoy parties and business meetings, but after a while wish they were home in their pajamas. They prefer to devote their social energies to close friends, colleagues, and family."[1] She was describing at least a part of me to a tee.

One day I was sharing with a friend how I don't seem to fit into the introvert *or* extrovert box. Sure, I love a good party, but I also enjoy long mornings alone or one-on-one conversations. I told her about some research I'd stumbled across, how two-thirds of us don't identify as introverts or extroverts.[2] My friend asked me if I'd heard of the term *ambivert*. I had not. She explained that an ambivert is "a person whose personality has a balance of extrovert and introvert features," and suggested that this definition better described me. Despite the oddness of the word, it aptly describes me. Give me extroversion without the hours of small-talk. Give me introversion without the cloistered cave.

WE ALL NEED QUIET

Whether we call ourselves extroverts, introverts, or ambiverts, all of us need quiet—times when we pause, reflect, and assess. In fact, this was a truth Jesus lived. He modeled quiet throughout his ministry. For instance, just after he was baptized, the Spirit of God led him into the wilderness for forty days of quiet, and at the end of that season, he beat back the temptation of Satan and pushed into his public ministry. After many of his miracle-making moments, Jesus retreated into the mountains for solitude and prayer. On the night before the crucifixion, Jesus spent time in quiet reflection and prayer in the Garden of Gethsemane. Quiet was a part of his consistent routine—so how much more must *we* need it in our own lives? We would do well to understand that we are able to be our best selves when we are centered in a place of quiet rest.

But if you think getting quiet is easy, think again. You'll have to fight the entire culture for it. The noise and distractions are endless in this digital age. Even if you clear out the distractions and create space for quiet, you'll have to get comfortable with yourself—with being alone with your thoughts, failures, hopes, dreams, wounds, and longings. For some of us, quiet can be the scariest place to go. But when we go there, when we establish routines of quiet and protect them, incredible things happen for our emotional and mental health.

First, in the quiet we gain perspective. When the noise of our lives overwhelms us, we often misconstrue or lose track of reality. By creating space away from our busy realities, we can see more clearly what is happening and gain new energy to approach the challenges that have nested too close to home.

Second, the quiet helps us become more emotionally resilient and empathetic to others. A recent *Forbes* article noted, "Studies show the ability to tolerate alone time has been linked to increased happiness, better life satisfaction, and improved stress management."[3] Quiet helps us maintain a sense of calm, re-center, and become more fully who we were designed to be.

Being quiet doesn't only benefit us. It helps us relate to others, too.

QUIET: THE WAY TO MAKE THE WORLD A BETTER PLACE

I incorporated intentional practices of quiet into my life, and as I did, I noticed improvements in the ways I interacted with the world. Quietness infused the way I related to others, enabled me to be a bearer of peace, love, and wisdom in in the midst of chaos. In fact, the more I pushed into the quiet, the more I was able to connect with the people in my life and become a better friend.

QUIETNESS INFUSED THE WAY I RELATED TO OTHERS,
ENABLED ME TO BE A BEARER OF PEACE, LOVE,
AND WISDOM IN IN THE MIDST OF CHAOS.

How?

The quiet taught me to **listen** again. As I did, I asked genuine questions of my friends. I stopped to connect with their hearts and hear their ache, and I learned how to extend empathy, pray for them, and be a better support. Quiet listening also taught me to **discern**. I began to hear what was *not* being said. I started to read between the lines, notice facial expressions, observe when the eyes shifted away if questions became too personal. Quiet discernment helped me see when someone was hurting, striving, or pushing too hard, and it led me to ask whether there was a need I could meet. Finally, quiet listening taught me to **understand**. It taught me how to keep from filling every empty space with words, taught me how to sit in quiet empathy for my spouse, friend, and children.[4] Quiet listening kept me from assuming and overreacting in defense, things which only hurt those closest to us.

A few weeks ago, my son Pierce and I went for a walk to catch up on how things were going for him. He was a couple months into his sophomore year, and his days were consumed with the constant demands of school sports, songwriting lessons, term papers and exams. Although he was grateful for it all, I heard his voice crack mid-sentence as he expressed that he was feeling pressured to measure up. Pierce usually manages stress with ease and maintains a light-hearted demeanor no matter the circumstance. I knew this was a unique moment not to solve or fix, but to lean in. So I paused and said, "Tell me more."

A conversation ensued in which he told me things I wouldn't have heard if other people were around or if we were hustling to and fro. My only responses were things like, "I'm so sorry you are facing this," Or, "I know how things can build up." I offered no answers. No solutions. By giving my son space and silence, I allowed him to receive what he really needed: to be loved, heard, and understood.

WHEN WE CARVE OUT SPACE FOR THE QUIET, TO RETREAT
TO A SILENT PLACE TO PRAY, JOURNAL, OR READ, WE
REST FROM THE NOISY DISTRACTIONS OF OUR LIVES.

When we carve out space for the quiet, to retreat to a silent place to pray, journal, or read, we rest from the noisy distractions of our lives. This rest pulls us out of the anxiety and stress of the world, if only for a moment. When we create spaces of quiet with others, it allows us to take a break from offering solutions or unwanted advice and allows us to show empathy, love, and understanding.

Quiet—it provides a refuge for ourselves and others from this noisy world.

⌁ REFLECTION QUESTIONS ⌁

1. CARVE OUT 15 MINUTES FOR QUIET REFLECTION. TAKE NOTE OF WHERE YOUR THOUGHTS GO WHEN YOU ARE ALL ALONE, WITHOUT ANY DISTRACTIONS.

2. WHEN WAS THE LAST TIME YOU SAT IN SILENCE? LIST WAYS YOU MIGHT INCORPORATE QUIET INTO YOUR WEEKLY RHYTHMS.

3. WHERE CAN YOU CARVE OUT THIRTY MINUTES TO AN HOUR OF QUIET IN YOUR DAILY RHYTHM, TIME TO REFLECT (AND BREATHE) WITHOUT ANY DISTRACTIONS?

DO THE HEART WORK

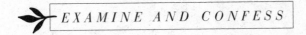 *EXAMINE AND CONFESS*

CHAPTER 4

DO THE HEART WORK

EXAMINE AND CONFESS

*God grant me the serenity to accept the things I
cannot change, courage to change the things I can,
and the wisdom to know the difference.*

—REINHOLD NIEBUHR

O ne fateful day in June, I found myself poring over volumes of
photos on my computer. I was on a tight project deadline, so
naturally, scrolling through the last seven years of photos seemed
like the perfect distraction. I flipped through each photo of our kids
in the Big Apple. How young they were! Kindergarten, second and
third grades. The boys had blond, moppy locks. Kennedy wore a
plaid headband and had our toy poodles, Trevi and Flora, in tow.
Tiny bodies dwarfed by bulging backpacks, they knelt to feed ducks
at our favorite Central Park pond or negotiated a free cupcake on
our daily commute home from school.

I savored the memory of those days, how each moment felt like an adventure as I dropped to their level, trying to capture the world through my children's eyes.

I scrolled ahead to a group of photos I didn't recognize, a series of scenes set in in the woods of Connecticut where our family had sought respite over a fall break. Our six-, eight-, and ten-year-olds had dreamed up the perfect kids-will-be-kids afternoon: a picnic by the woods on the edge of the front yard. They packed sandwiches, popcorn, and juice boxes, dragged out a patchwork snowflake quilt, Dr. Seuss books, the Rat-a-Tat Cat card game, a Grinch costume, a zebra hand puppet, and a T-ball set. Gabe had captured the entire experience on camera, lurking behind a curtain in the front office window. I'd had no idea.

Frame by frame, photo by photo, I watched the afternoon unfold in slow motion. One of the kids opted for a solo baseball game. Kennedy pitched and batted on her own. She threw the ball in the air and nailed it, her face awash with sheer determination and grit. Pierce examined a leaf up close, picked from a pile on the ground, then jumped up to cheer for his sister. Cade took their distractions as an opening to finish off lunch, sneaking crumbs to the poodles, who circled nearby.

The next photo caught me off guard. It was me. Head buried in my laptop, headphones on, laser-focused on writing my first book. These sacred moments of spontaneity had taken place in the front yard . . . and me? I had missed every second of it.

I zoomed in to see their facial expressions, pondering their person- alities. I was reminded of their innocence and wide-eyed wonder. They would follow Daddy and Mama anywhere, and we certainly took them up on it. I remember saying in that season how resilient kids were, and the truth is, they really were resilient—until they weren't.

I looked again at the photo of me, hair wild, rumpled sweatshirt, typing away, all in the name of being diligent. What other moments had I missed, head buried in my work? Year after year, I couldn't possibly be present for everyone. But this felt different. I hadn't felt the weight of missing out until I saw it in retrospect, in vivid color from a long-past October day.

Until you get quiet, you can't know what your heart needs to confess.

In that room, seven years later, I fell to my knees in tears. These toddlers-turned-teens, now taller than I, weren't in that carefree season anymore, and they never would be. They now carried stress and loads of responsibility: deadlines, social cues, high school transcripts. I wanted to crawl back through the lens, and relive that afternoon. I wanted to change it all, walk away from my computer and pitch to Kennedy, collect leaves with Pierce, and tease Cade for feeding his last bite of sandwich to the dogs.

I suppose most parents live with the question, *What more could I have done?* And in that moment, the question came calling for me. I'd worked through one memory only to remember others: the nights I skipped tuck-ins and called up from the bottom stair. In my worst moments, I'd ignored my children's pleas. Stared at my phone. I wanted to feel the weight of these things, to grieve what was lost, to acknowledge my ignorance.

Grateful for this insight, I considered a new question: *What can I do now?* This is where things begin to change.

HOW TO KEEP A CLEAN HEART

I knew that if we sit in regret too long, if we let it swirl without release, we descend into a rabbit hole of shame. We nurse guilt. So often, our regret, shame, and self-condemnation do not motivate us to be more present, more proactive. Instead, they lead to more anxiety and defeat.

Confession to God, on the other hand, allows us to begin again and make today count. Tonight, even. Every pause is a chance to release and reset. Peace cannot happen without the discipline of self-examination. When we pause long enough to examine our hearts, to confess to God where we have messed up, cleansing happens.

> YOU CANNOT HEAL WHAT IS HIDDEN, BUT WHEN YOU CONFESS SOMETHING OUT LOUD, YOU BRING IT INTO THE LIGHT, WHERE IT CAN BE HEALED.

These things are true: **You cannot heal what is hidden**, but when you confess something out loud, you bring it into the light, where it can be healed. The power of guilt and shame has no hold on you any longer, because **secrets lose power when they exit the dark.**[1]

Here are three questions to ask yourself to kick-start the heart work. They will walk you through confession and toward change (which is the path of true repentance).

1. **What do I need to confess?** Heart work begins with awakening, like what happened to me the afternoon I explored my photo library. When my awareness of moments I'd

missed brought deep shame and guilt, I confessed my tendency to allow work time to spill over into family time.

2. **What do I need to release?** Nursing guilt shows a fundamental distrust of God's forgiveness, healing, and restorative power. Once we confess, we release our guilt to God, and trust that he will work through our failures to bring about his purposes.[2]

3. **What do I need to change?** Confession and release paves the way for how we can walk forward in new, more connected and present ways. Keep asking God, "What can I do now?" His plans and purposes will continue to unfold.

After we do the heart work and amend our ways, we have a path forward that's free from guilt, shame, and anxiety. We've reflected, confessed, and begun to walk in a new way. A better way. Guilt and shame keep us trapped in cycles of anxiety, depression, perhaps even panic. The only consistent way I've found rest from these cycles is to keep my heart clean through confession, release, and forgiveness.

Confession is the gateway to freedom. Freedom is the beauty of forgiveness.

Allow me to provide a word of caution: When you start doing the heart work, you might stumble upon some pretty big things. Old wounds. Deep pains. Perhaps even some dark patterns of behavior. If this is the case, don't try to carry those burdens alone. Find a counselor, therapist, pastor, or priest to help you carry the load. Though I'd recommend a professional guide to help you navigate these issues, it might not be a bad idea to pull a trusted and willing friend into the mix, too.

CONFESSION IS THE GATEWAY TO FREEDOM.
FREEDOM IS THE BEAUTY OF FORGIVENESS.

The Proverbs writer penned these words: "Above all else, guard your heart, for everything you do flows from it."[3] Let's do the heart work: examine and confess, forgive and release, then enter our communities and the world beyond as healing agents.

⇗ REFLECTION QUESTIONS ⇖

1. ASK YOURSELF: WHAT DO I NEED TO CONFESS? ARE THERE ACTIONS OR INACTIONS THAT I'VE AVOIDED EXAMINING, THINGS I'VE FAILED TO CONFESS BECAUSE OF GUILT OR SHAME?

2. WHEN IS THE LAST TIME YOU PRACTICED CONFESSION WITH A COUNSELOR, PASTOR, PRIEST, OR EVEN A FRIEND?

3. SIT IN A QUIET PLACE AND TAKE INVENTORY. WHAT CAUSES YOU GUILT, SHAME, STRESS, OR ANXIETY? RELEASE IT TO GOD AND ASK HIM TO BRING YOU PEACE.

COUNT
SHEEP

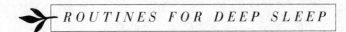
ROUTINES FOR DEEP SLEEP

CHAPTER 5

COUNT SHEEP

ROUTINES FOR DEEP SLEEP

*Finish each day and be done with it. You have done
what you could. Some blunders and absurdities
no doubt crept in; forget them as soon as you can.
Tomorrow is a new day. You shall begin it serenely
and with too high a spirit to be encumbered with
your old nonsense.*

—RALPH WALDO EMERSON

My daddy was a night owl. Many a night I remember him rev-
ving up the popcorn machine, ready for conversation with
anyone who would listen, while I stumbled off to bed. After twelve
hours of high school, band practice, and homework, I couldn't hang.
Dad seemed to thrive when everyone else was asleep; he'd whip up
something in the kitchen, listen to the radio, or read a book into the
early morning hours. But his lack of sleep caught up with him each

day by late afternoon, when he sometimes dozed off mid-sentence while sitting upright.

I never was a night owl, at least not until my first pregnancy at the age of twenty-five. With my swollen belly, tiny bladder, and need to spoon a king-size pillow on my left side, I got my first taste of insomnia. I chalked it up to pregnancy, but when Cade came, my sleepless nights continued. I'm sure feeding a newborn every three hours had something to do with this.

As our family expanded, so did my sleepless season. Babies two and three came, and I slept even less. Five years into parenthood, I realized a new groove had been carved in my brain. My body was programmed to wake every night around three a.m., even if the children didn't wake me.

Some nights I'd wake to use the bathroom and drift back to sleep. Other nights, my mind would rush to what I didn't accomplish the day prior, and I'd create a mental task list. Sometimes I woke with conviction, mulling over how I could have treated someone differently, replaying the conversation in my mind. On rare occasions, I'd pull way out and take a broader inventory, examining and questioning the current season: *Was I living well? Loving well? Focused on what matters?* These racing questions seemed of utmost importance in those pre-dawn hours, and I always had the energy to process each topic. I'd reach for my phone to capture my conclusions on the notes app so I could reference them later.

WAS I LIVING WELL? LOVING WELL?
FOCUSED ON WHAT MATTERS?

As the years progressed, my mid-sleep musings became more spiritually productive. I'd feel prompted to pray, or consider a Scripture I'd use for an upcoming talk, or remember a story for a writing project. Instead of treating these moments of being jarred awake as a nuisance, I began to assume these interruptions were *invitations* to encounter something I wasn't making time for during the day.

I accepted my new normal, sleeping only half the night, and even though I was always exhausted, I learned how to navigate my life at 60 percent. With an extra shot of caffeine mid-afternoon, and half a Tylenol PM in the evening, I could rally and make my lack of sleep work, at least when I wasn't traveling.

For what seemed like too many months in a row, I traveled early and often. I scheduled too many pre-dawn flights, stayed up too late talking with women after events, half-slept in random hotel rooms, and had no real rhythm. When I returned to my family, I had no energy left for them. By the time the kids arrived home from school each afternoon, I felt like I'd been hit by a train. I wanted to crawl into bed, wanted to tell my kids, "I know I haven't seen you all day, but I'm dead tired." The shame I felt from shortchanging them pushed me to forge ahead—with a headache and short fuse.

Because I wasn't getting enough rest, everything felt overwhelming. Even the simplest tasks—loading the dishwasher, sorting laundry, writing an email—felt like an uphill slog through molasses. During this sleepless season, dirty clothes and dishes were piled high. Gabe picked up the pieces, which added its own dynamic of stress. The more responsibility I took on, the less I slept. The less I slept, the less productive I was. The less productive I was, the more helpless I felt. Helplessness brought stress, anxiety, and mild depression. My relationships with those I loved most began to suffer, and in the meltdown of it all, I began to feel like the purpose I had fought for was being stolen by the sandman.

That's when I knew: it was time to get serious about sleep.

CREATING THE CONDITIONS FOR SLEEP

I started researching sleep, and I realized just how important it was. One Harvard study claimed, "lack of adequate sleep can affect judgment, mood, ability to learn and retain information, and may increase the risk of serious accidents and injury."[1] What's more, the report suggested sleep deprivation could lead to health problems and even early mortality. If there was one thing I didn't want, it was to die early, so I got even more serious and read even more about sleep.

In her book *The Sleep Revolution*, Arianna Huffington reports, "when you find depression, even when you find anxiety, when you scratch the surface 80 to 90 percent of the time you find a sleep problem as well."[2] Huffington shows how sleep deprivation isn't just an adult problem, either. In fact, it is exacerbated in teens: "Television, video games, smartphones, tablets have all been recently identified as agents that frequently disrupt a child's sleep, including leading to total sleep deprivation."[3]

Getting enough sleep is critical if we hope to experience sustained emotional and mental health. And though we'd all like to have night after night of great sleep, we're often unaware of the simple factors contributing to our lack of rest. Huffington helped me understand these, too. Her book helped me see the need to make sleep a top priority, and I began implementing some of her suggestions for creating an environment for better sleep. I started turning down the lights at the end of the evening and tried to create a sense of calm in the bedroom prior to getting in bed. I did my best to keep devices away from the bed and kept my bedroom temperature below seventy degrees. I began taking baths before bed and lighting candles. I even wrote down things I needed to do so I wouldn't wake with a mental list hours later. Those things seemed to help, but it was only the beginning.

I created a consistent structure for organizing my time each day. I spent the morning hours doing creative work and held meetings over lunch. In the afternoon, I tended to correspondence and then took a brisk walk. As I became more intentional about the rhythm of my days, I fell into bed, content with a day spent well. Instead of stressing with regret and seeing a mountain of things undone, I went to bed tired and with a heart of release—the perfect way to drift off to sleep. When I got intentional about my waking hours, my sleeping hours followed without interruption.

I started eating better, too. I cut sugar down to a bare minimum, especially after dinner. I offset my sugar intake with plenty of exercise, no less than 10,000 steps a day. This seemed to help, too, and the more I slept, the more energy I had to keep this new cycle of sleep going. For the first time in years, I was enjoying sleep. In fact, I started looking forward to it. As I caught up on years of missed sleep and reset my rhythms, I began to notice the effect on my life. I was more productive and able to keep up with the important tasks of each day. My mood was better, too; my fuse not as short with Gabe or the children. I began to see *sleep* as the reward for a well-lived day. *Sleep* was the invitation, not the mid-night wakeup call, and as I slept more and more, I could sense the anxiety, stress, and chaos of my internal world melting away.

> WHEN I GOT INTENTIONAL ABOUT MY WAKING HOURS, MY
> SLEEPING HOURS FOLLOWED WITHOUT INTERRUPTION.

Does low-grade anxiety or depression follow you everywhere you go? Are you often distracted, unable to follow a singular train of thought? Is your temper often short? Do you lose it on your coworkers, kids, and spouse daily? Dig a little. Ask yourself, *Am I getting enough sleep?* If you're not getting between seven and nine hours, change up your rhythms and routines, and make sleep a priority. It'll make all the difference.

⟱ REFLECTION QUESTIONS ⟰

1. HOW MANY HOURS OF SLEEP DO YOU GET A NIGHT? IF IT'S LESS THAN SEVEN, WHY?

2. WHAT IS YOUR BEDTIME ROUTINE? HOW MIGHT YOU CREATE A SENSE OF CALM BEFORE CLIMBING INTO BED?

3. COMMIT TO MAKING SLEEP A PRIORITY. WRITE A LIST OF
   THINGS YOU'LL DO TO MAKE SURE YOU'RE WINDING DOWN
   BEFORE YOU CRAWL INTO BED. THEN, CHOOSE YOUR BEDTIME
   AND WAKE-UP TIME AND STICK WITH IT.

MORNING ROUTINE

 COFFEE, CANDLE, AND A PEN

CHAPTER 6

MORNING ROUTINE

COFFEE, CANDLE, AND A PEN

The first hour of the morning is the rudder of the day.

—HENRY WARD BEECHER

Early mornings are my favorite. It wasn't always this way. For years I rebelled against the six a.m. alarm of my youth. But as a mama of a toddler and teens, I'm now the first to wake, usually a few moments before dawn. I love when the house is hushed and reverent, and on the days I'm fortunate enough to catch the first glow of orange on the eastern horizon, I smile. I believe God grins back. Even when I've had a week wherein I can't seem to get it right, Jesus is near.

Each morning, coffee brews, the comforting cadence of hot water dripping through freshly ground beans echoing in the empty kitchen. When it's finished, I pour the coffee into a sealed tumbler to keep it hot as long as possible. I light a candle or start a fire, depending on the season. If it's cold, I'll spread a thick blanket in front of the fire and quiet my heart as I kneel in child's pose, arms extended over my head, palms up.

A dog-eared book of liturgies is on our coffee table, gifted to us this past Christmas. Many mornings I whisper my favorite passage from Douglas McKelvey's *Every Moment Holy*, to center my mind and heart.

> Meet me, O Christ, in this stillness of morning.
> Move me, O Spirit, to quiet my heart.
> Mend me, O Father, from yesterday's harms.
> From the discords of yesterday, resurrect my peace.
> From the discouragement of yesterday, resurrect my hope.
> From the weariness of yesterday, resurrect my strength.
> From the doubts of yesterday, resurrect my faith.
> From the wounds of yesterday, resurrect my love.
> Let me enter this new day, aware of my need,
> and awake to your grace, O Lord. Amen.[1]

Once here, in God's presence, I feel no urgency to leave, as the prayers flow freely. I ask, listen, and wait. There's no other place to be, naked and honest, but before the heart of our Father. In those moments, God sees our all, before the daily chaos and confusion, before any fear or delusion. There, he bends low to meet us in our intention. He gives strength to help us push through it all.

If possible, I start every day this way. Prayer grants me access to the Holy Spirit's comfort, a balm that transcends time and space, reputation and race. Through these moments, Jesus repairs, restores, redeems, and resurrects.

My morning routine starts with prayer because it leads me to comfort and shields me from the world's spin cycle of striving, stress, and anxiety. It roots my day in fullness instead of scarcity. When I'm well-rooted, I then turn to my journal.

PRAYER GRANTS ME ACCESS TO THE HOLY
SPIRIT'S COMFORT, A BALM THAT TRANSCENDS
TIME AND SPACE, REPUTATION AND RACE.

We all journal in different ways, I suppose, but often, I'll scratch out my ongoing dialogue with God. Each entry begins with the setting, the time, the date. As much as these entries help me discern the direction of any given day, I know they'll serve as reminders of God's faithfulness in the days to come. (My journal collection stretches back more than a decade.)

I don't stop with prayer and journaling, though. Each morning, I turn to God's Word, which nourishes my soul and fills me up after the previous day's pouring out. Through the Scriptures, I learn who he's made me to be. I learn how to live a life that looks more like Christ's. I learn how to love others—Gabe, my family, the world around me—well.

How do I approach the Bible? Each day is a little different. Sometimes I take a passage and camp there, or a long section of Psalms, sometimes an entire book at a time in the Old or New Testament. But each day, this time in the Scriptures is like the table set by God in Psalm 23. It's a feast the Father has laid out for me, offering me everything I will need as I set out for the rest of the day.

The last step of my morning routine is gratitude—giving thanks. It's a practice that's grown out of my time reading Scripture. The summer before I wrote this book, old worries began haunting me; I felt stress and anxiety setting in. But one morning, I woke with these words on my lips: "Do not be anxious about anything, but in every situation, by prayer and petition, with thanksgiving, present your requests to God. And the peace of God, which transcends all understanding, will guard your hearts and your minds in Christ Jesus."[2] As I spent time in God's Word, I sensed the Holy Spirit inviting me to lay down my anxieties and to give thanks for the deliverance he was bringing, even if I couldn't see it yet. And so I began my daily intention to offer thanks—thanks for the things that already happened, the things that were happening, and the things that would come. Culminating my morning routine with a short gratitude list and a closing prayer of thanks, I emerge ready to face the day.

MAKING SPACE FOR THE COMFORTER

I think of what Jesus said to his disciples in the upper room in what I like to call his "great commencement speech." Over the course of that long meal, he washed his disciples' feet, served them Communion, and told them everything they were going to need to know when the time came for him to return to his Father. This would be their last meal together before his arrest and crucifixion.

One of the six things he promised his followers was the gift of the Holy Spirit, the comforter and advocate. I think of this every time I create a space for God in my quiet moments before dawn. Sometimes I begin the day overcome by grief, by insecurity, by discouragement, by loneliness, and all I want is to get on my knees and plead for grace and healing. There are days I need to process my failures from the day before. Sometimes I need encouragement for the day ahead. No matter the situation, though, I begin the morning anticipating a meeting with the Holy Spirit, the one who brings whatever comfort and direction I need. Even in my moments of tearful confession, he's there.

God promises to be our comforter and help, but we have to give him an opportunity to do just that. If we don't make space for him, if we don't build it into our routine, how will he meet us where we need him most?

WHAT'S YOUR MORNING ROUTINE?

A morning routine sets the framework for our day. When we begin our days by spending time with God, with his comfort, his pace, his timing, it brings healing. There's no script, no race, no rules. There's only peace, courage, and strength for the day ahead.

GOD PROMISES TO BE OUR COMFORTER AND HELP, BUT WE HAVE TO GIVE HIM AN OPPORTUNITY TO DO JUST THAT.

What's your morning routine? Do you drag yourself out of bed late, slog through a rushed and harried process of getting out the door and entering into the demands of the day? Or do you take it more slowly, settle into God's rhythm, and let his comfort dictate the pace? If you find yourself in the former camp, consider making a shift. Get more sleep the night before so you wake bright-eyed, ready to spend time with your Creator. Meet him with expectation, ready to hear from him. Meet him in prayer, in journaling, in the Scriptures, in gratitude. As you meet him, expect him to bring comfort to your anxiety.

↗ REFLECTION QUESTIONS ↖

1. HOW DOES YOUR TYPICAL MORNING BEGIN? IS YOUR MORNING ROUTINE HURRIED AND HUSTLED, OR DOES IT BEGIN IN THE PEACE AND CALM OF TIME WITH GOD?

2. HOW DO YOU PRACTICE GRATITUDE? IF THIS ISN'T PART OF YOUR DAILY ROUTINE, TAKE SOME TIME RIGHT NOW TO EXPRESS YOUR THANKS TO GOD.

3. IF YOU BELIEVED YOU COULD START EACH MORNING IN THE COMFORT OF GOD, HOW WOULD YOU PRIORITIZE YOUR TIME TO MAKE THAT A REALITY?

STOP THE WORK

PRACTICE SABBATH

CHAPTER 7

CHAPTER 7

STOP THE WORK

PRACTICE SABBATH

*A world without a Sabbath would be like a man
without a smile, like a summer without flowers, and
like a homestead without a garden. It is the most
joyous day of the week.*

—HENRY WARD BEECHER

A s the Friday sun began to set in Jerusalem, the Wailing Wall
was crowded with devoted families offering final prayers
before dusk. A few moments later, we walked from the Old City
toward our dinner destination, hearing festive sounds fill the air,
from children playing in the streets to men scurrying home before
sundown. The sun settled, the noise dissipated, and peacefulness
settled in. But our night was just about to begin.

A group of friends and I were visiting the Holy Land for the first time, enveloped by an old world with rich sights and smells to offer to our modern one. At the end of our fifteen-minute walk, we entered a home where we were greeted by our warm and friendly hosts, new friends who'd invited us to experience a traditional *Shabbat* dinner (Hebrew for Sabbath).

After a ceremonial prayer of blessing, we feasted on several courses of delicious fare, including challah, baked salmon, hummus, golden beets, grilled eggplant, roast chicken, and ribeye with rosemary baked potatoes. With readings, candles, and songs, the couple invited us into their rich tradition. Each course brimmed with bounty and meaning. I felt drawn into their Hebrew culture, grateful for the experience of embracing the Sabbath with reverence, intention, and joy.

I considered the words written by the prophet Isaiah and how our new neighbors were enjoying the fruit of his counsel:

> "If you watch your step on the Sabbath
> > and don't use my holy day for personal advantage,
> If you treat the Sabbath as a day of joy,
> > GOD's holy day as a celebration,
> If you honor it by refusing 'business as usual,'
> > making money, running here and there—
> Then you'll be free to enjoy GOD!
> > Oh, I'll make you ride high and soar above it all.
> I'll make you feast on the inheritance of your ancestor Jacob."
> > Yes! GOD says so!"[1]

I had just walked into a true Sabbath—in Jerusalem, of all places! Right in the middle of the streets where Jesus walked, we experienced a profound evening, one I will never forget.

SABBATH AS A VERB

If there is one rhythm we can embrace after learning how to take time for rest, it's this one. We must Sabbath. This practice is essential for our ability to grow in mental, emotional, and spiritual health. We cannot run if we cannot rest. If we infuse all the other habits into our lives and fail to do this, everything else is at risk.

The English word *Sabbath* is derived from the Hebrew word *Shabbat*, the day God commanded the Jewish people to rest. They were to stop work from Friday sundown through Saturday sunset. This day was to forever be their day of rest, a symbolic and living reminder of how even God rested after completing six days of creation.

WE CANNOT RUN IF WE CANNOT REST.

Taking a rest isn't a sign of weakness. Yet our culture whispers the opposite: if we try harder, work smarter, make the right career moves, get that next degree, work overtime, connect with influencers, and go for our dreams, we just might live a life of significance. But God declares we are *already* chosen, beloved, appointed, and set apart. He ordered our lives with purpose and intention. We don't need to hustle to prove something God says is already true.

Your value as a human being isn't found in *what you produce*; it's found in *who you are in Christ*—a person designed in the image of God to glorify him forever. From the beginning, God designed his creation to be more abundant, fulfilled, and joyful when we work from a place of rest and renewal.

Scripture is replete with examples of God bringing this rhythm of rest and renewal into all of creation. He led by example, creating the world in six days and resting on the seventh.[2] In Exodus 23:12, the Scriptures state, "Six days do your work, but on the seventh day do not work, so that your ox and your donkey may rest, and so that the slave born in your household and the foreigner living among you may be refreshed."

But even if you don't hold to the Christian or Jewish faith, science backs up the brilliance of this God-ordained rhythm. For example, farmers know to give their fields a rest every few years in order to restore nutrients to the soil for maximum growth.[3] When they allow a field to lie fallow for one year, the following six years produce abundantly more than if they had tried to keep the field productive that seventh year. When we intentionally Sabbath—stop striving so much—we create space for healing, wholeness, and refreshment. It's a truth built into the design of all things.

HOW TO CREATE A RHYTHM OF SABBATH

So how might keeping the Sabbath become a part of your daily, weekly, monthly and annual rhythm?

Our Jewish friends take the Sabbath seriously and plan ahead. I can appreciate their resolve. They buy their groceries, prep their meals, finish their work, and anticipate Friday evenings. When the sun hits the horizon, they are ready! They enjoy those twenty-four hours to the full, setting aside all work, purchases, and productivity. This allocated time is precious and critical to the life, health, and vibrancy of their community.

For most of us, however, constant demands, schedules, travel, and to-do's make it almost impossible to create a perfect Sabbath rhythm. What works for one person or family may not work for others. Still, you can do your best to be intentional about rest and renewal. After all, if it doesn't make it on your calendar, Sabbath rest won't happen at all.

The practice of Sabbath doesn't need to be restricted to just a weekly rhythm. You can develop a plan for a quarterly and annual practice as well. These patterns of pause help ensure your life, family, and relationships are receiving the life-giving benefits of uninterrupted time.

Here's how Gabe and I try to do this.

Each week we take time over breakfast or lunch to stop the work and focus on our relationship. Every once in awhile, we have an extended date night. We also make sure to have at least one "family night" planned on the weekend, usually a late afternoon and evening dedicated to just the six of us. We set aside anything digital and spend our time together playing a board game, sitting around the fire and singing songs, or having karaoke dance parties. Most weekends, we take a family walk in the woods, something I learned from Eugene Peterson, who described his family hikes as an essential part of his Sabbath rhythm.[4]

Quarterly, we make time for the two of us to take a full day away. This isn't always possible because of our schedules and responsibilities, but we've found that when we step away together and reconnect, re-centering our focus on our goals, we get critical perspective as we stop to consider and express how each of us is *really* doing.

Annually, Gabe and I try to get away for a few days or a long weekend to take time just for us. His parents helped make this possible when the kids were young, and now we try to schedule our getaway while our kids are at summer camp. During these times of rest and renewal, Gabe has opened his heart to me in ways I never imagined possible—and likely would not have without these sustained days of alone time. Stopping the work gives our marriage an annual reset. These days are magic for us. Our conversations go deeper than we seem to ever get in the bustle of life. We get beneath the surface and to the interiors of our hearts.

If you don't have family who can take your kids for a few days, and if summer camps are out of the question, another solution might be swapping childcare with trusted friends for a weekend overnight. We did this when our children were young. Our kids loved that they were able to have a slumber party with their friends, and the adults were happy to swap one night of having double the kids for a night without any kids.

We also have an annual Sabbath rhythm for our entire family. During December and July, we put aside work travel and intentionally spend time together as a family. We might take an overnight trip somewhere a couple of hours away or a family vacation. Most of the time we stay local and schedule consistent nights and weekends of hikes, concerts, bike rides, ball games, mini golf, movies, and, of course, a progressive tour of Nashville's favorite eats. Our children know that even when these months are busy, Gabe and I set aside uninterrupted time for our family to be together. By building this rhythm into our annual calendar, we stay grounded in a plan that gives life to each member of our family.

This practice of Sabbath rest is often neglected in this harried age. Yet if you want to maintain your emotional, physical, and spiritual health, it's important to reconnect with yourself, God, your family, and your community. But Sabbath—both on a particular day of the week and on a planned, multi-day basis—can allow us the space we need to understand our lives are not rooted in work, productivity, or acquisition. Our worth is found in the God who loves us, who created rest for our good.

Are you finding ways to practice Sabbath? If not, take a moment to plan how you'll make space for Sabbath over the coming months. As you practice, ask yourself, "Is this rest freeing me from the typical anxieties of our bustling world?" If your experience is anything like mine, the results will speak for themselves.

↗ REFLECTION QUESTIONS ↖

1. WHAT KEEPS YOU FROM SETTING ASIDE A PARTICULAR DAY TO SABBATH?

2. WHAT ARE THE BARRIERS THAT KEEP YOU FROM A DAY OF REST? IS IT YOUR WORK? THE PRESSURES OF EXTRACURRICULAR OBLIGATIONS? BE SPECIFIC.

3. HOW MIGHT PRACTICING SABBATH BE BENEFICIAL FOR YOU AND YOUR FAMILY?

RESTORE

The rhythm of rest is the foundation of renewal. Without rest, we'll teeter on the edge of burnout and struggle to meet the demands of life with Spirit-infused energy. However, once we embrace a consistent rhythm of rest, we find the potential to be **restored**—the input rhythm we'll talk about next. Restoration replenishes us physically, fortifies our mental health, and enables us to engage emotionally.

To restore is "to bring back to a state of health, soundness, or vigor, to put back to a former place, or to a former position."[1] Synonyms include *restart, refresh, repair,* and *rejuvenation.*

One of my favorite passages in Scripture about restoration is Isaiah 58:11–12:

> I'll give you a full life in the emptiest of places—
>> firm muscles, strong bones.
> You'll be like a well-watered garden,

a gurgling spring that never runs dry.
You'll use the old rubble of past lives to build anew,
rebuild the foundations from out of your past.
You'll be known as those who can fix anything,
restore old ruins, rebuild and renovate,
make the community livable again. (MSG)

What a vision.

We are in desperate need of restoration. The hustle and bustle of life keeps us in constant motion, consequently wearing down our bodies, minds, and spirits. At the same time, as our bodies, minds, and spirits are being depleted, we're also hearing a clear message from society that we should discard something once it's worn out and used up, and replace it with something new.

See the problem? We can't head over to Amazon and buy a new body, mind, or spirit. We can't consume our way out of burnout. Instead, we have to restore the gifts God's given us, the gifts of our bodies, minds, and souls.

God did not create us to participate in the world's wear-down cycle, the culture of constant consumption that leads to so much unrest. Instead, he made us to engage in regular rhythms of physical, intellectual, emotional, and spiritual restoration, rhythms that pull us out of the world's churning and fill us (and the world around us) with life.

INSTEAD, WE HAVE TO RESTORE THE GIFTS GOD'S GIVEN US, THE GIFTS OF OUR BODIES, MINDS, AND SOULS.

In this section we'll be reminded of who God says we are and of his promise to restore. We'll learn ways to reestablish a full life; to eat smart, push ourselves, and build firm muscles and strong bones. We'll find the fullness of adventure and play and talk about how to sharpen our minds. When we submit to these rhythms of restoration for our bodies, minds, and spirits, we find new mental energy and emotional strength in the midst of the wear-down cycle of the world.

How can we be restored? Let's find out.

PERMISSION TO PLAY

GIVING UP CONTROL

CHAPTER 8

PERMISSION TO PLAY

GIVING UP CONTROL

It is a happy talent to know how to play.

—RALPH WALDO EMERSON

I woke at four in the morning, hustled out the door, jumped in an Uber, and made my way to Chicago's O'Hare airport. In a drowsy stupor, dozing on and off in the back of the car, I reflected on the past few months. I'd just finished my fourteenth trip in less than twelve weeks, and there were still two left before the holidays. But before those last two events, Gabe and I would have a break, a gathering with dear friends on a ranch in Sedalia, Colorado, and boy, did I need it. I was managing too many things—my travel logistics, study, writing, speaking, and my family—often hundreds of miles away. I'd hit a wall of fatigue. I was ready to be free of it all, to have some fun. This weekend was just what the doctor ordered.

I landed in Denver and set out on the two-hour journey to a mountain haven. About halfway there, Gabe called and greeted me, informing me that I would be arriving just about the time the group was setting out for a horseback ride on the ridgetop trail. Did I want to join them? I'd had only four hours of sleep the night before (and four the night before that) and crashing on a bed in the cabin sounded more appealing than jumping on a horse. But I knew this was a rare opportunity for me to play, so I said yes.

The driver dropped me off at the barn, where the wrangler met me, fit my saddle, and offered a list of ride options from beginner to advanced. I'm not a skilled equestrian, so I requested the moderate, middle-of-the-road ride. "Horses can smell fear a mile away," our guide said as he eased me into the saddle on my horse, Amigo, and I settled in. I took a deep breath and patted my brown companion on the side of his neck. "We're going to have a great day," I whispered in his ear.

As we headed out on the trail, the wrangler began with the basics. I relearned how to steer, walk, and then post a trot. The autumn air was crisp, the sky bright blue as we practiced over and over in a wide-open field. The wrangler was patient with me, and as I grew more comfortable on the back of my horse, I began to unclench my fists and squeeze with my legs. As I released my death grip on the saddle horn and relaxed, my excitement grew.

The wrangler decided I was ready to try out a lope, a full-on run the likes of which you'd see in a western movie (and not what I consider "moderate" ride territory). Despite my protests, he wouldn't let me off the hook: "Trust me, you'll love it," he said.

Love it? Yeah, right.

As we picked up the pace, I felt out of control, which is the *worst* feeling for a not-yet-recovered control freak. Almost falling off the side of the horse, I yelled, "Stop!" Unlike trotting, which requires you to *do* something, to manage something, loping, apparently, is the opposite. The guide told me that when loping, I needed to allow the horse to carry the responsibility while I relaxed in the saddle. I nodded, still uneasy. Just before the horse took off the second time, I whispered a prayer: *God, please remove all fear today. I want to enjoy your creation, as a daughter, wild and free. Replace the fear with joy!*

Amigo picked up speed, and as I relaxed into the three-beat cadences, my right arm flung out wide like a rodeo girl. The wind blew through my hair. The sunlight was warm on my cheeks, and I was smiling. A smile? Wow! It was in that realization that I began gut laughing. Full-on, joyful laughter. I'd given over my need to control and was able to experience the beauty of this wild animal running free. It was exhilarating! It was freedom!

By the time we finished the ride, Amigo and I were besties. I was already anticipating the next day's lope on my trusty steed. But that night, after a hearty dinner of lamb and wild rice, the head wrangler stopped by our table to tell me he'd already promised Amigo to someone else the following day. I was crushed. Amigo was *my* horse, the horse that helped me overcome my nerves.

The next day, I was given Newcastle, a gray-and-white horse with the sweetest disposition. We set off, slow and lazy up the mountain, the head wrangler leading a group of four of us up on the high ridge. He rode a horse that had bucked a wrangler the day prior in front of an entire group, and I was riding right behind that horse, heading up a steep mountain on trails no wider than a footprint. What would happen if his horse got spooked? Would mine, too?

Anxiety crept in. How many ways could this go wrong? Could my horse lose his footing and slide down the mountain? Could he buck me and throw me down the mountain?

I went to battle, and moment by moment, I put on my brave face and did my best to muster courage. I'd always believed this simple definition of bravery: Bravery is moving scared. So I prayed again, *God you know how much I desire to enjoy your creation, and yesterday offered hope. Help me release these what-ifs. Help me release my tendency to control or manage. Cover me in peace to enjoy every part of this ride.*

BRAVERY IS MOVING SCARED.

After that prayer, I made a conscious decision: I'd have confidence that God had control of it all, and I'd allow that truth to help me relax. So while we made our way up the mountain, I kept my mind at ease by bantering with the couple beside me. We shared stories of parenting, marriage, and the outdoors. I stopped focusing on fear or control and settled into the journey, and when we approached the top of the mountain, it was time to lope again, and with extra instruction, off we went. I relaxed my body again, settled into the groove, right hand flying out to steady me. After a couple more loping runs, I was grinning widely again.

Up on the top of the mountain ridge, after a smattering of glorious pictures, the wrangler asked with a twinkle in his eye, "Are you ready to run long and fast?" My heart skipped. Of course I was. Though fear threatened, a surge of confidence pushed it aside. *Let's do this!* We loped for what felt like the longest of runs, twisting and turning along the top of the mountain ridge, picking up the pace. I whooped and hollered, released into the crazy, hoping it'd never end.

What joy, to run wild and free! If this was what playing feels like, I'd like more. The ride swept me back to my childhood, before the need for control took over, before I learned to be afraid. When I had no shortage of confidence or imagination. When I invited bite-sized acts of courage into everyday play.

PLAY AND CONTROL CANNOT COEXIST.

As I've reflected on my experience at the ranch, I've come away with a few lessons. Among them is this: Play and control cannot coexist. Afraid of taking a risk, of losing control, I often miss opportunities for play, which is a shame because it's play that breaks us out of our stressful routines and rejuvenates us. It's play that so often restores our freedom and joy.

THE IMPORTANCE OF PLAY

The importance of play for children is well documented. We assume kids should play, but adults? Aren't we supposed to be mature, responsible grown-ups? That's how so many of us live, but researchers are now documenting the benefits of play for adults and finding that "play isn't just about goofing off; it can also be an important means of reducing stress and contributing to overall well-being."[1] Lynn Barnett, a researcher and professor of recreation, sports, and tourism at the University of Illinois at Urbana-Champaign wrote, "Highly playful adults feel the same stressors as anyone else, but they appear to experience and react to them differently, allowing stressors to roll off more easily than those who are less playful."[2] Her research study concluded that playfulness in adults contributes to their resilience, one of the great attributes needed to cope with 21st century demands and stress.[3]

Let's be honest: playing feels childish, to me anyway. But I've come to see that the practice of play is critical. Why? Because it forces us to give up control. Our tendency is to push against the release of control—control of work, control of relationships, control of family, control of logistics, control of fear, control of whatever. After all, isn't managing our lives what it means to be an adult? So we hold on tight, but our death grip just leads to more anxiety, more stress.

MAKING SPACE FOR PLAY

Play can become our instructor if we'll let it. We can allow play to show us that everything won't fall apart when we let go and give ourselves a little space and freedom. As we do, we'll find the stress and anxiety of management and control melting away, if only for a while. But if this is going to be a reality in our lives, we need to pray for the courage to become like children again. If we do, we'll find that childlike freedom—from stress, anxiety, and moments of affliction—has been waiting for us all along. While the stressors may not go away, we can develop a rhythm that helps us become more resilient to deal with them.

What are you trying to control or manage? Can you name it? Does it bring stress into your life? Today, even if just for a few minutes, find ways to release control and management and give yourself to frivolous play. Consider a fun family board game or, if you have one, a family jump on the trampoline. Pick up a musical instrument to play for fun, or make a family band—that's what we do. Between a guitar, ukulele, and a band in a box, everyone in our family gets an instrument. We also keep a karaoke machine in our living room. It has an attached disco ball that will strobe lights across the ceiling to the beat of the music. Our kids keep that thing pumping with solo acts and a microphone stand.

For play that needs more than a moment's notice, grab your tennis racket or make your way to a pool and take a jump off the high diving board. Mount a horse, if you have a local stable, or throw a frisbee in your front yard. Whatever it is, take the time to play and see if you don't find relief and rejuvenation from letting go, releasing control, and experiencing a little lope of your own. See if it doesn't refresh you, restore your mind, and give you new energy to enter back into a busy world.

⤴ REFLECTION QUESTIONS ⤶

1. HOW MUCH TIME DO YOU CARVE OUT EACH WEEK FOR PLAY?

2. WHEN WAS THE LAST TIME YOU TOOK AN INTENTIONAL BREAK FROM WORK TO PLAY SOMETHING—A GAME OF PICK-UP BASKETBALL, A BOARD GAME, ANYTHING? WHAT IMPACT DID PLAYING HAVE ON YOU?

3. DO YOU HAVE ANY TIMES OF PLAY SCHEDULED IN THE NEXT WEEK? IF NOT, CARVE OUT SOME TIME AND PICK A PLAY ACTIVITY TO ENGAGE IN. FOR BONUS POINTS, MAKE SURE IT'S *COMPLETELY* FRIVOLOUS.

EAT
SMART

CHAPTER 9

EAT SMART

BRAIN FOOD

One cannot think well, love well, sleep well, if one has not dined well.

—VIRGINIA WOOLF

My first body-conscious memory is from seventh grade. I was in PE class, wearing the shortest of shorts made of navy polyester. I had to run a mile in those scratchy shorts in the scorching Florida sun that day. I rounded the football field on the fourth lap, my inner thighs chafing and burning against each other. *What is happening? Why are my legs rubbing together and burning?* I wondered. This was long before I understood the concept of a thigh gap.

I wasn't used to wearing such revealing shorts. I grew up in a conservative home where culottes were substituted for shorts. Perhaps you've heard of culottes? When a skirt wants to be both shorts and pants and all parties seem to be okay with that? Culottes were so special and rare, one could only acquire these billowy knee-length wonders by making them at home on the sewing machine via tissue-paper pattern, hand-cut fabric, and a healthy dose of patience. I had a special lavender pair, which were passed between me and my homeschool friends in the next town over. We squeezed every bit of life out of those beauties.

But that day with the shorty-short scratchy shorts? Something clicked in my brain. My legs were not okay. I started looking at everyone else's legs: they were long, lean, and muscular. How had I never noticed this before? How could I get a pair of those? Something needed to change.

On the outside, the shift wasn't obvious, but I made up for it behind the scenes. I changed my clothes in the bathroom when everyone else used the locker room. I began to weigh myself regularly on my mom's bathroom scale when no one was around. I'd squeeze in extra runs. But I still loved sweets. My girlfriends would order cakes from the Publix bakery each weekend before band competitions. We'd sit in a circle, forks in hand, eating from the box like it was our last meal. I just made sure to burn those calories afterward, even if it meant a late-night run.

During my freshman year of college, Krispy Kreme opened near my campus. My roommates and I made it a nightly ritual to grab a dozen donuts for the dorm whenever the "hot" sign was on. To compound my sugar addiction, I stashed Little Debbie Swiss rolls under my bottom bunk. To no one's surprise but mine, I gained twenty pounds in three months. Over Christmas break, Mom's bathroom scale didn't lie, so I ramped up the running, counted every calorie, and lost those pounds by the end of spring semester.

By my sophomore year, the Krispy-Kreme-Little-Debbie season was long forgotten. People commented, "Rebekah, you never struggle with weight." Or did I? I monitored everything that entered my mouth. If I ate one gummy bear, I followed it with twenty jumping jacks. When I waited tables at Applebee's, I snuck just a few fries at the end of the shift. And then? I worked out. Carb load; workout. Carb load; workout. This was my rhythm. In all honesty, I can't remember eating vegetables in college.

When Gabe and I first married, we made our home in the South. Between sweet tea and the daily temptation of southern cuisine, our workout routines began to wane. We started "Family Nights" every Tuesday, a weekly potluck of yellow-shaded casseroles, each representing a vegetable with crackers and cheese on top. For dessert, the crowd favorite was the appropriately named Dump Cake, as heavy as it sounds. Made of cake (made from a box), covered with pie filling (from a can) and drizzles of butter, topped with ice cream. (Are you salivating yet?) Fortunately, I birthed three babies in that season, and used my pregnancies as an excuse to eat whatever felt right.

You can't eat unhealthy forever, though; sooner or later it'll catch up with you.

It all came to a head for me two years ago, when my energy level plummeted and I started getting nagging headaches. My anxiety and depression started to rear its ugly head too, and the number on the scale crept up. I'd been trying to juggle tweens and a career that required writing deadlines with a great deal of travel, leaving my adrenals crashing upon returning home from each trip. More than anything, I wanted to be mentally and physically strong. I wanted to have energy. I didn't want to have headaches. I wanted the mood swings to settle down, and I didn't want the anxiety and attendant panic to come roaring back.

I was willing to try anything.

I knew I couldn't keep crawling back into bed out of sheer exhaustion at three p.m. when the kids were arriving home from school. I couldn't be up for countless nights in a row with insomnia. I couldn't keep skipping workouts out of lack of strength. Something had to change. Unlike before, it wasn't the width of my thighs that motivated me to make a change this time. It was understanding this: *it doesn't matter what the outside reveals if the inside is starved of strength.*

I've never been one for extreme diets, but I read the intro to a Whole30 book and decided to start the plan right then and there—to eliminate sugar, grains, legumes, soy, and dairy from my options for the next thirty days. It was July, so I had the margin for extra grocery runs and time in the kitchen. I even made my own mayo (twice) and tried to follow all the rules. I reached out on Instagram asking for tips and advice, and was so encouraged by the responses. Others had done this. I could, too. So I pressed on.

IT DOESN'T MATTER WHAT THE OUTSIDE REVEALS
IF THE INSIDE IS STARVED OF STRENGTH.

For the first time in twenty-five years, I went without half-and-half and sugar in my coffee. I also started eating vegetables without crackers and cheese, and come to find out, they're delicious if you roast them with olive oil and sea salt. I'd also never cooked with citrus, and found that a little freshly squeezed lemon, orange peel, or lemon zest made every veggie turn a cartwheel in my mouth. Then I discovered all those A's: avocados, almonds, acaí bowls! The flavors of these foods spoke to me and told me something I was ready to hear. The best food for your body is delicious!

As I turned over a new dietary leaf (a lettuce leaf, to be exact), I found that eating healthy fuels your brain, which in turns regulates your emotional and mental state. What's more, I learned that science backs up my experience. One study noted, "[serotonin] is a neurotransmitter that helps regulate sleep and appetite, mediate moods, and inhibit pain. Since about 95% of your serotonin is produced in your gastrointestinal tract . . . lined with a hundred million nerve cells, or neurons, it makes sense that the inner workings of your digestive system don't just help you digest food, but also guide your emotions."[1] In fact, multiple studies have found a correlation between a diet high in refined sugars and impaired brain function, and even a worsening of symptoms of mood disorders, such as depression.[2]

While doing Whole30, my mental outlook was restored. I was sharper, more focused. I had more energy. I felt good, and I found that when my body felt good, my outlook and attitude was more positive, brighter, and I was better able to remain strong and hope-filled, even when stress started to press in. When I loved myself enough to prioritize healthy foods for my body, love carried over to every other area of my life.

MAKING A MENU FOR HEALTHY EATING

Researchers are continuing to explore the correlation between eating and mental health. This work is urgent, in no small measure because our children and adolescents are experiencing increased feelings of depression. With the onset of anxiety and mood disorders beginning in children between six and thirteen years old,[3] it's critical for parents to establish healthy eating patterns for their children. But what American family has extra time in their lives these days? When we're busy, taking time to cook a healthy meal is often the first thing to go. I know because that's how it is for me. Even to this day, I have my cheeseburger moments. I'll find myself in the car, frantic like any other mom, flying between swim team and golf practice and YoungLife, with a sudden urge for Sonic. But when I cheat and skip eating clean, I pay for it. My body reacts, my brain reacts. So does Gabe's. So do my kids'. On these occasions, I'm reminded why I must stay the course.

What do I do to get back on track? I go back to the recipe box in our kitchen, pull out our go-to healthy family favorites, make a meal plan for the following week, and stock the fridge by Sunday. Here's what I've learned: without intentional planning, a healthy menu can be difficult to maintain. For me, thirty days of clean eating was enough to forge a new groove. My grocery list changed; a new rhythm was established. I didn't want to go back to the old ways. My palate had changed, too, and I desired savory over sweet. To this day, I haven't gone back to coffee with half-and-half and sugar. It's going to be almond or coconut milk for our family from here on out. We still love our sweets but are trying to be smarter in our choices. Dark chocolate with almonds and sea salt on a regular basis, and cookies or cakes with healthier ingredients for something special.

PICK A PLAN, ANY PLAN

The good news is that many people are assessing their eating and changing their habits out of a desperate need to feel more alive and to overcome the symptoms of poor physical and mental health. Many of us are spurning the harmful ingredients and food processing practices that became mainstream over the last few decades, and we're replacing them with healthier eating plans like Whole30, keto, Mediterranean, gluten-free, or vegetarian diets.

THE SAME CREATOR WHO MADE OUR BODIES TO TICK,
TO FUNCTION, TO BE STRONG, AND TO THINK ALSO
MADE FOOD TO REPAIR, REJUVENATE, AND RESTORE US.

Which plan you choose isn't as important as making the choice to only eat food that is closest to the way it was when it came from the ground, because the same Creator who made our bodies to tick, to function, to be strong, and to think also made food to repair, rejuvenate, and restore us.

So if you're struggling with your health, if your mental state is off, if you're plagued with anxiety, stress, or lethargy, ask yourself: *Might the foods I eat be contributing to this feeling of disease and dis-ease?* If they are, try a different approach. Try thirty days of intentional eating, eating the way our Creator meant for us to eat. If you notice a difference, make healthy eating a daily part of your rhythm of restoration.

↗ REFLECTION QUESTIONS ↖

1. WRITE DOWN THE FOODS YOU ATE IN THE LAST THREE MEALS AND NOTE HOW MANY FRESH VEGETABLES AND FRUIT YOU CONSUMED. HOW HEALTHY IS YOUR TYPICAL DIET?

2. WE ALL KNOW OUR DIETS COULD BE BETTER, BUT WHAT'S ONE CHANGE YOU COULD MAKE TO CREATE HEALTHIER PATTERNS OF EATING?

3. WHEN YOU EAT HEALTHIER, WHAT DIFFERENCE DOES IT MAKE IN HOW YOU FEEL PHYSICALLY, EMOTIONALLY, AND MENTALLY?

KNOW YOUR IDENTITY

LABELS DON'T DEFINE YOU

CHAPTER 10

KNOW YOUR IDENTITY

LABELS DON'T DEFINE YOU

Once you label me you negate me.

—SØREN KIERKEGAARD

"Mom, what is Down syndrome?" Pierce asked with tear-stained, chubby cheeks after exiting the bus one autumn day in second grade. The term for his brother's medical diagnosis had yet to surface in our home. We weren't in denial as parents; we simply wanted our younger two to know their brother for all he is, as Cade.

Growing up with a sibling who has different needs comes with its own unique set of responsibilities, a tender-hearted-protector type of calling. Pierce, being the middle child, had been pushed into the role of the eldest, even when it wasn't natural for him. But he always embraced this responsibility with compassionate zeal.

When Pierce and Kennedy were in first grade and pre-K, friends might notice something different about Cade and ask them about it. Questions like, why didn't Cade talk as much, or why he was slower to write words or understand a game? In "big" brother fashion, Pierce would respond, "That's Cade. He learns differently than some kids. Sometimes he just needs extra time." This seemed to satisfy the curious observers. After all, those inquiring were often children of our family friends, and regardless of his comprehension, they'd always known Cade as happy, great at dancing and hugs, all of which earned high praise in toddlerland.

Things took a turn when we moved to New York City.

That autumn day, Pierce continued, "These boys at school were making fun of Cade. They called him retarded and dumb, and my usual answer wasn't good enough for them."

A tear crept out of the corner of my eye.

I hugged his little neck and reassured him. "Honey, I'm sorry," I said. "Those kids don't know Cade, so don't listen to them. I'm so proud of you for standing up for your big brother."

"But Mom, that's not all. A girl tried to help defend Cade and talked about how he had Down syndrome. What's Down syndrome?

A memory flashed before my mind's eye: the day I told a dear friend in Atlanta of Cade's confirmed diagnosis. With tears in her eyes, Amy prayed for the day I'd first explain to Cade's future younger siblings why he was different. Now I was fielding a pointed question from Pierce, age seven, and I knew today was that day.

I called Kennedy in and gathered both kids close. I explained that Down syndrome is a diagnosis given to children who have an extra chromosome, one more than the rest of us. I told them Cade's particular diagnosis of trisomy 21 develops four to six days after conception—before I even knew I was pregnant. But all these details weren't what our kids were after. They had a bigger question on their minds: Was something *wrong* with Cade?

Wanting to give these brave hearts the answers they needed, I paused for a silent prayer and then continued, "From the first week Cade started growing in my tummy, God saw a different future for him. He knew this little boy might act and appear a bit different to others, but in the best kind of way, his unique perspective would remind us of what is most important in life and love."

I shared with them the psalmist's words in Scripture: "For you created my inmost being, you knit me together in my mother's womb. I praise you because I am fearfully and wonderfully made. Your works are wonderful, I know that full well."[1]

ONCE YOU KNOW SOMEONE, YOU
NO LONGER LABEL THEM.

I told them the label "Down syndrome" was a way of explaining to the world how Cade's body works, but it doesn't define Cade. Cade is Cade. He got his love for music and left-handed writing from his mama, his love to party and his thick head of hair from his dad. I told them that if they found the term helpful, they could use it, but the most important thing was to help their friends grow in their relationship with Cade.

This felt right. To capstone the moment, I asked, "Aren't we glad God saw fit to let us be his family?" Without hesitation, both kids nodded in vigorous support.

Once you know someone, you no longer label them.

THE POWER OF A LABEL

I've been struck by how many conversations revolve around our labels. "I'm ADD, OCD, manic, depressed, disabled, handicapped, diabetic . . ." The list goes on and on. We throw out labels as if they clarify who we are, maybe even our most defining marks. We use these descriptors as a way of helping people keep their expectations of us in order. The problem is, when we use one of these labels to describe ourselves, they often give us our deepest sense of identity. We believe the lie that the label defines us. We shift from believing a particular label is *something we face* to believing it's *someone we are*.

This sets up expectations of an indefinite future with a predetermined outcome. Yes, I know Cade's cell division in my womb won't un-divide when he turns eighteen, but cell division doesn't determine Cade's future. His life can be just as rewarding as anyone else's: full of vision, education, positivity, love, and hope. And he can bring education, positivity, love, and hope to everyone he encounters.

Labels are powerful things we can misconstrue as our identities. But what if we came to understand that labels don't define us? That, instead, they are an explanation to help the world understand things we've dealt with or come up against? When we don't view our identity through a label, we're able to find ways to thrive in spite of whatever label we are living under. This mindset helps us turn from despair to hope in action.

When I faced panic attacks eight years ago, I didn't have a diagnosis for what was happening. Looking back, it was a grace because this kept me from giving myself a label that I could make part of my identity and give up thinking I could live any other way. Instead, I tried new approaches to try and overcome my fear of being trapped in tight spaces. Each day I prayed for a heavy dose of peace and courage, and then tried to push through my claustrophobia via exposure. I continued to approach subways, elevators, and crowds, scary as it was. Some days I was successful, and some days I'd retreat. But the game-changer was learning who Christ really made me to be and discovering my true identity.

MY PAIN BECAME MY PURPOSE.

Over time, the small spaces lost their scariness. I didn't hesitate to hop on an elevator or a subway train. And although my panic attacks began years ago on an airplane, I now hop on an airplane on many Fridays in order to share the healing journey of these rhythms with people around the country. The irony is not lost on me. My pain became my purpose.

WHO ARE WE REALLY?

Today, 76 percent of us believe we best "define ourselves" by looking within.[2] That is, if we stare deep into our psyches and evaluate our feelings, personalities, passions, desires, and even addictions long enough, we will discover our true selves. But looking only at ourselves can bring disillusionment and lead us to an empty place. Why? Because though our internal realities are true, they don't *define* us. They don't always show us who we really are. After all, isn't the self always growing? Isn't the soul oriented toward God always changing on its journey to eternity? Staring into a mirror might show us what we look like in the moment, but it cannot show us who we are or where we're going.

So how do we find our true identity, who we are and where we're going? The Christian faith leads us beyond the trappings of ourselves and into an identity rooted in something more solid, more immovable—God himself. Identity in him is trustworthy and unchanging.

When our identity is found in who God says we are rather than in our highs and lows, our successes and failures, or our desires, affections, or shortcomings, we experience the freedom we were meant to enjoy. When I need to be reminded of this, I read this list of phrases that tell me the truth about who God says I am, and it always helps:

I am a child of God. (John 1:12)

I am a new creation. (2 Corinthians 5:17)

I am a friend of Jesus. (John 15:15)

I am created by God to do good. (Ephesians 2:10)

I am free in Christ. (Galatians 5:1)

I am chosen and loved. (1 Thessalonians 1:4)

I am the light of the world. (Matthew 5:14)

I am not ruled by fear. (2 Timothy 1:7)

I am forgiven. (Colossians 2:13)

I am God's possession. (Titus 2:14)

I am free from the desires of the flesh. (Galatians 5:24)

I am a light in the world. (Matthew 5:14–15)

I am secure in him. (1 Peter 1:3–5)

I am loved by God. (1 John 4:10)

If you have worn your own identity label like a name tag, take a moment to ask God who you are in him. Root yourself deep in that identity. Then, with an identity rooted in the God who gives wisdom, strength, and love, go out into the world, secure and confident in who you really are.

⇗ REFLECTION QUESTIONS ⇖

1. WHAT ARE THE LABELS YOU'VE BEEN GIVEN, THE ONES YOU LIVE UNDER? HOW MIGHT YOUR LIFE BE DIFFERENT IF YOU SHIFTED HOW YOU TALK ABOUT YOURSELF AND THE THINGS YOU FACE? FOR EXAMPLE, INSTEAD OF SAYING THINGS LIKE "I AM . . ." YOU START SAYING, "I'VE WALKED THE ROAD OF . . ." OR "I'VE STRUGGLED WITH . . ."

2. IN WHAT WAYS DOES GOD'S DESCRIPTION OF YOU DIFFER FROM THE LABELS YOU'VE TAKEN ON?

3. WHAT AREAS OF PAIN IN YOUR LIFE SHOW GLIMPSES OF PURPOSE? WRITE DOWN WAYS YOUR JOURNEY CAN BECOME AN ENCOURAGEMENT TO SOMEONE ELSE.

TAKE A WALK

CLEAR THE BRAIN FOG

CHAPTER 11

CHAPTER 11

TAKE A WALK

CLEAR THE BRAIN FOG

Methinks that the moment my legs begin to move, my thoughts begin to flow.

—HENRY DAVID THOREAU

It was the third Monday in January of 2005, a dull, gray morning in the suburbs of Atlanta—a grayness that described my weeks-long mood. I backed our minivan out of the garage, willing myself to drive to the grocery store and Target. I'd reward myself afterward with a coffee drive-through, a make-it-til-naptime pick-me-up.

Once the kids were settled in their beds with books and blankies, I opened my laptop to look up the definition of a term I'd heard on the radio, "Seasonal Affective Disorder." According to the internet, this diagnosis (often known as SAD) "is a type of depression that comes and goes with the seasons, typically starting in the late fall and early winter and going away during the spring and summer."[1]

One article led to the next, and as I read, I discovered SAD is often the worst on "Blue Monday," a day falling about one month after Christmas and often coined the "most depressing day of the year." Looking back, I could see how I'd been through a few Blue Mondays of my own, though I hadn't realized it. Its proper name was derived from a seasonal convergence of several factors: poor weather, dreary outlooks, Christmas debt, the reality of failed New Year's resolutions, and so on. I was right in the thick of it, researching SAD on the saddest day of the year. As I did, I felt a sort of relief that I wasn't alone in my depression on this Blue Monday. As I read on, relief set in as I realized that as the blooms erupted in April, my heart would swell happily again.

A few months after that Blue Monday, we moved to New York City. We sold 75 percent of our possessions and relocated to an apartment on the Upper East Side. With all the transition this move required, I had yet to consider the shift in what would be my primary mode of transportation: from the car to my legs. Trading a suburban life for a pedestrian one would have a greater effect on my heart than I could imagine.

Snow flurries swirled outside our apartment windows on Halloween, just four months after the move. I looked up toward the window from making goodie bags for our new neighborhood friends, nervous about a pending season of cold starting this early. But we were in the north, after all. With all the change, the shift in weather, the daily navigation of a new city, I couldn't fathom adding depression to the mix. But the season was arriving, whether I was ready or not, and I'd need to face it.

One month into that dreadful winter, I found myself walking outside to the gym in eleven-degree weather, surprised by the spring in my step. There was something nice about the brisk air against my cheeks. I thought to myself, *Maybe it wasn't the winter that brought the sadness. Maybe it was my suburban inactivity.* Our life in New York didn't allow for that. Without the option of going from my kitchen to my garage to the car, I had to use my actual legs and burn some energy.

—————

WALKING HELPED IMPROVE MY MENTAL AND
EMOTIONAL HEALTH, AND I DON'T MEAN WALKING
FROM MY BED TO THE FRIDGE FOR A MIDNIGHT
SNACK. I MEAN WALKING LIKE IT'S MY JOB.

—————

I found the perfect comrade for forays into the Manhattan winters, a coat designed for below-freezing temps. With all excuses ruled out, I found it wasn't all that hard to get around.

If I had a meeting? I had to walk.

If I wanted to go the grocery store? I had to walk.

Pick up the kids from school? Walk.

A vanilla latte? Walk.

Even in the dead of winter, those walks lifted my spirits. Creative ideas emerged. I jotted down unexpected thoughts on my phone. I didn't experience any hint of Seasonal Affective Disorder that winter, or during any winter since. I was learning something profound. Walking helped improve my mental and emotional health, and I don't mean walking from my bed to the fridge for a midnight snack. I mean walking like it's my job.

GETTING INTENTIONAL ABOUT WALKING

The average person now spends 9.3 hours sitting per day—far more than the 7.7 hours we spend sleeping.[2] This inactivity is creating a set of cascading issues that can undermine our other attempts to get out of our funks. Not only does the lack of exercise make us more susceptible to heart disease, Type 2 diabetes, and other ailments that come from a lethargic lifestyle, but it's shutting down our brains and limiting our growth.

You might be surprised to know that several of the most innovative people in modern history saw walking as essential to their daily rhythms. From Steve Jobs to Sigmund Freud, walking was a way they carried on meetings and processed their best thinking and advice. Even in the 1800s, Charles Dickens walked almost twenty miles every day to de-stress and free his mind to come back fresh for composition.[3] In fact, because it has been determined that walking helps us think better, Google has incorporated "walking meetings" into its workday. Employees can reserve the time they want to meet on the indoor walking track.

But most of us don't live in New York City or work in places like Google, so we have to be intentional if we want to incorporate walking into our days. After we moved to Tennessee, one of my greatest concerns was how it was going to affect my walking pattern. After all, the pedestrian lifestyle of New York birthed my writing career and inspired my creativity, and I knew maintaining a walking lifestyle would require intention now that we were back to driving around Franklin. If I didn't want to settle back into the suburban temptations of comfort and conformed lethargy, I'd need to be strategic.

So Gabe and I made a plan. Daily, we'd get out as a family to Harlinsdale Farm or walk the paths of Carnton. I'd hike the trails of Lake Radnor with girlfriends or walk the dogs in our neighborhood while Cade rode his bike. Whenever I could, I'd take the stairs. Excited about what walking was spurring for our family, I got my daughter a Fitbit that Christmas. It had a modern, white band and rose gold clasp, and whenever she forgot to wear it to school, I "borrowed" it. I found that as my step count increased, my productivity increased, too. I smiled more.

INSTEAD OF RUNNING FROM PAIN, WALK THROUGH IT

When my dad died in April, my baby sister and her son came to visit. We never left the house, except to take long walks or hike in the woods. It connected us to Dad, how he loved the outdoors. On the trail, leaves crunching under our feet, we pointed out what Dad would have loved about those spring woods, pregnant with life. He would have beamed, wild-eyed like a kid in a candy store, describing every plant we passed. I watched my nephew pick up a leaf in wonder, wave it from the stem, then laugh in delight. Like Poppy, like grandson.

When the sadness of death still lingered at April's end, I worried depression would come calling in May. Apparently, there's not a time limit on grief. With more healing to come, I told a friend I didn't want to hemorrhage in public, so I got quiet instead. Some days all I knew to do to keep the sadness from sinking me was to count my steps.

Walking became a way to work through my grief, and because I'm a verbal processor, I prayed prayers of surrender while I walked. Anyone who passed me may have thought I was crazy, but I didn't care. For me, walking was freeing. Looking back, walking was the best way to care for my heart. Sometimes through worship, sometimes through a whisper, sometimes through silence, God met me while I walked. Day after day, each time I turned back toward home, my heart felt a bit lighter again.

By summer the grief lifted, creativity emerged, and much of the time, my most innovative ideas came while walking. Day after day, I found the cobwebs clearing. Ideas took their place. Walking and writing began to go hand in hand; I almost couldn't tap out a paragraph without a good walk beforehand. Even today, before I began writing more about this particular rhythm, I went on a long hike through the woods with Gabe. We caught up on the happenings from the past three days while he had been out of town. I told him what I'd been listening to, what I'd been writing, what I'd been learning about this rhythm before penning these words. That walk (combined with Gabe's probing questions and brilliant insights), kickstarted this chapter.

WALK INTO CREATIVITY

I'm not the only one who's noticed a connection between creativity and walking. While writing this book, Gabe and I visited the home of a friend and mentor who also happens to be the author of several bestselling books. He's one of the most efficient and effective people we know, always working on a project but never sacrificing the essential life rhythms. In his mid-fifties and fit as a whistle, he told us of the key to his output over the last decade. As we went downstairs, he opened the door to his office and in front of a panoramic window was a treadmill desk. A treadmill desk? Yes, you read that correctly. Just over the control panel of a typical treadmill sat a long desk that held notes, books, pens, and his laptop. He walked and wrote. Over ten thousand steps a day at 2.0 mph, writing away. Talk about strategic walking! I was hooked on the idea.

One Wednesday a few weeks later, I arrived home after a long day of meetings, overwhelmed by the looming writing deadlines ahead of me. Gabe took my hand and walked me up the stairs. There, my new friend "Nancy the NordicTrack," awaited. My husband had bought and assembled my very own treadmill desk and placed her in the perfect spot, in front of a large window overlooking a long, pastoral view, and he'd done it without me knowing. It felt like Christmas morning. I'd get to write the majority of this book on the move!

As I type even now, I'm walking in place. When I need a break to think, I look up and out. It's raining outside. There's a stream running from the back of the yard downhill through the front to the street. My thoughts clear, and I get back to work.

WALKING THE PATH TO RESTORATION

Walking is critical for the restoration of our mental health, creativity, and productivity. When seasons of grief hit, when I've hit a wall with creativity, when I've run out of words, the best thing I can do is get out and walk. The movement offers release of control, allows the unforced connections to emerge. It gets my blood flowing, releases endorphins, and lifts my mood. Time and time again, walking brings clarity.

If walking isn't a part of your daily routine, you're missing out on a key rhythm of restoration, one that can pull you from the doldrums, bring new insights, and kickstart your creativity. How can you add walking into your daily rhythms? How can you make it a natural part of your life? Ask yourself these questions, then do a little brainstorming. Where should you do that brainstorming? On a walk, of course. Give it a try. See what happens.

⌁ REFLECTION QUESTIONS ⌁

1. ON A SCALE OF 1–10, 1 BEING A COUCH POTATO AND 10 BEING A DAILY WALKING COMMUTER, HOW WOULD YOU SCORE YOURSELF AS A WALKER?

2. WHERE CAN YOU GO TO TAKE A WALK? NAME A SPECIFIC PLACE LIKE A PARK, A GYM, OR AROUND YOUR NEIGHBORHOOD.

3. WALK FOR TEN MINUTES A DAY THIS WEEK, AND TAKE NOTE
   OF THE THOUGHTS THAT COME AS YOU WALK. AT THE END
   OF THE WEEK, REVIEW YOUR NOTES. WHAT DO YOU NOTICE
   ABOUT YOUR WEEK OF WALKING?

SEEK ADVENTURE

TAKE A TRIP

CHAPTER 12

SEEK ADVENTURE

TAKE A TRIP

> *Every day God invites us on the same kind of*
> *adventure. It's not a trip where He sends us a rigid*
> *itinerary, He simply invites us. God asks what it is*
> *He's made us to love, what it is that captures our*
> *attention, what feeds that deep indescribable need of*
> *our souls to experience the richness of the world He*
> *made. And then, leaning over us, He whispers, "Let's*
> *go do that together."*
>
> —BOB GOFF

A year ago, Gabe and I marked our twentieth year of marriage with a celebratory trip to Europe. Pierce and Kennedy were booked for two-week-long camps, and Cade was heading to the grandparents, so it seemed like the perfect time to get away. After teary good-byes, we made our way to the airport. The time away felt like a honeymoon, except this time, it didn't include spending a night on my aunt's sleeper sofa during our eighteen-hour road trip from Virginia to Miami to board a Christmas honeymoon cruise—but that's another story.

It had been six months since the bathroom-locked-in-panic-attack, and I hadn't locked any airplane bathroom door since. The space was too tight. I'd flown often and kept thinking I'd finally risk two minutes of trepidation, but each time, my neurosis won. So instead of locking the door, I'd jam my foot against it, hold the lever, and play tug-of-war with a confused passenger wondering why the green sign on the door read "Vacant." Then, when I was finished, I'd wash up and look down as I made the walk of shame back to my seat. But on this flight across the Atlantic, it was time. I knew in our coming travels we'd face heights and tight spaces and adventure, and I didn't want fear to steal any moment from our anniversary trip. This was my chance to test my courage.

Entering the bathroom, I locked and unlocked the door to make sure the mechanism wasn't broken. Then, in a rush of bravery, I locked it, hurried, washed up, and turned to the door. The latching mechanism slid with ease, and I made it out alive. *Whew!* Maybe it was a baby milestone, but with it, my courage grew.

We woke the next morning to a misty rain in Lauterbrunnen, Switzerland. We'd planned a rigorous hike in the Alps for our first day to get the blood flowing. I skipped out of the hotel with confidence, feeling brave from the airplane bathroom lock success. The natural next step of courage would be a hike in the Alps, but of course I didn't quite think through the requirements. To get to the trailhead, halfway up the mountain, we'd need a different form of transportation. After we scooped up our tickets at the counter and headed up an escalator, we came upon a platform with a glass box—a green gondola—ready to soar high in the sky.

This glass box was approximately twenty feet long and ten feet wide, with what seemed like fifty people jammed inside, and it was suspended in the air by a mere cable. Of course, we'd be the last to get on, and it appeared we'd be squished against the glass doors. It was so tight, I thought I might need to suck in just so the doors could shut.

Gabe, recognizing the situation, looked at me and asked, "You want to wait thirty minutes for the next shuttle? I'm happy to wait. But there's no guarantee there will be less people on the next round." My mind raced, recalling countless other times in the last seven years I'd jumped off overcrowded elevators and subways before the doors closed, my confidence evaporating. Tears began to well in the corners of my eyes.

I took a deep breath and responded, "I can't let this moment throw me backwards. I need this to be a week wherein I am brave. I cannot miss these moments because I'm gripped with fear. Let's do this." So we moved fast and stood on the edge of that glass cage. I held my breath as the doors slammed shut. As the tram began to lift, I tuned out the *oohs* and *ahhhs* of the crowd as they looked out over the valley. I whispered Jesus' name the entire time. If bravery is moving scared, this was the only way I knew to keep going.

As we approached the mountain ridge platform, I felt the exhilaration of relief. We shot from that glass box like a cannon, courageous and free! The ensuing hike was glorious; we pranced alongside a herd of cows adorned with cowbells, danced with locals to tunes from an Irish folk band, and stumbled upon a charming cottage restaurant with a piping hot brunch of muesli, eggs, and bacon served with a variety of pastries. Taking in these majestic mountain moments felt extra special due to my bravery. Little steps of courage gave way to a week of adventure.

Following our stay in Switzerland, we rented a car and ventured onto the road. We didn't have a specific plan in mind, just a few cities we wanted to land in over the course of the next several days. We set off to see what we could discover.

We drove through Geneva during the 500th anniversary of the Protestant Reformation and visited St. Pierre's Cathedral, where John Calvin spent the last twenty-three years of his ministry, for a little learning and architectural review (this is Gabe's idea of an adventure). We drove through the Mont Blanc tunnel from France into Italy, pulling off to the side of the road to take in the glacier waterfalls and surrounding beauty. We explored waterfront cities and marinas like Italy's Portofino, ate the best basil and tomato caprese crostini, and concluded each day with an evening walk for gelato. We climbed rocks and jumped off cliffs and swam in the Mediterranean. We walked the streets of all five Cinque Terre towns and even rented a speedboat at Lake Como for some fun in the sun. It was a very active, thrilling, magical week.

Looking back, I've wondered, *Why did those two weeks feel so alive for me, for both of us?* Of all the trips Gabe and I have taken, this one felt different. Granted, this particular trip was unique. We came into the week already emotionally connected as a couple instead of playing catch-up. Other years we'd use a quick getaway to reconnect, but in reality, two or three days can't always enliven a relationship operating with a deficit. Instead of needing this trip to process months of miscues without interruption, we had more time for fun, adventure, and play. As it turns out, fun and laughter was part of how we first fell in love twenty-two years ago, and it was just what we needed to be reminded of at this stage of life.

But there was more. Early on, from the airplane to the glass gondola, I'd determined to not be overcome by fear. So I stepped into adventure. Sure, I locked the bathroom door in an airplane and boarded a gondola, but I also walked down a dark village street and climbed behind waterfalls and walked closer to the edge of cliffs. (Maybe those things sound like mini-adventures for some of you, but for me, they required an extra measure of bravery.)

HOW INTENTIONAL ADVENTURE
BEATS BACK FEAR

We all know fear is one of the greatest threats to mental and emotional health. It sends us into fits of anxiety and panic. But instead of avoiding the things we fear, we might consider confronting them. Gregory Berns, a leading neuroscientist, writes in his book *Iconoclast*: "Although fear is the great inhibitor of action, its location in the brain is well known . . . rather than people needing to avoid the situations that cause fear or the circumstances that make them stress out, neuroscience is showing how the rational part of the brain can regain control over such toxic emotions like fear."[1]

Fear holds us back and keeps us believing the lie that we aren't strong enough, brave enough, or mentally tough enough to break out of our ruts, even when we know better. But by reminding ourselves of the truth (this elevator won't fall to the ground; there's nothing to worry about in this small space) and pushing into adventure, we can regain control over fear. When that happens, instead of avoiding potentially stressful situations, we begin to run toward them and see them as a challenge to overcome.

Berns says, "To see things differently than other people, the most effective solution is to bombard the brain with things it has never encountered before. Novelty releases the perceptual process from the shackles of past experience and forces the brain to make new judgments."[2] In other words, when I put myself in new situations, even when they require fitting into tight spaces (like the gondola), and I see the *reward* of those situations, my brain cultivates new ways of seeing the world. Ways that aren't rooted in the efficacy of fear.

CHOOSE YOUR OWN ADVENTURE

Our two weeks in Switzerland and Italy were filled with novelty and adventure. New sights, new sounds, new foods, new interactions—all of which stirred my curiosity and imagination. Not only did I replace old memories of fear with new moments of courage, I also replaced old experiences of avoidance with new moments of pressing in.

IF WE ARE CREATIVE BEINGS, DEPENDENT ON
IMAGINATION, DOESN'T IT RING TRUE THAT WHEN
WE FOSTER NEW EXPERIENCES, WE'LL FEEL ALIVE?

If we are creative beings, dependent on imagination, doesn't it ring true that when we foster new experiences, we'll feel alive? You may not be able to work in a trip to Europe anytime soon, but what if you decided in the next day, week, or month to take a mini-adventure? Anything can be made into an adventure—but it usually requires a little extra time and a willingness to risk and discover something new. Take your family or a few friends for a weekend camping expedition. Visit a local art gallery, or go on an architecture tour of your city. Set out to expose yourself to new things, especially if the adventure requires you to overcome a fear or two.

⌐ REFLECTION QUESTIONS ⌐

1. WHAT FEARS OR ANXIETIES DO YOU NEED TO OVERCOME? MAKE A LIST.

2. WHAT ARE SOME INTENTIONAL WAYS YOU CAN CREATE AN ADVENTURE THAT REQUIRES YOU TO FACE AND OVERCOME YOUR FEARS?

3. WHEN IS THE LAST TIME YOU HAD AN ADVENTURE THAT
   INSPIRED CONFIDENCE OR FILLED YOU WITH COURAGE?
   DESCRIBE WHAT YOU DID AND HOW YOU FELT.

BREAK A SWEAT

SWEAT

USE THE WORKOUT PANTS

CHAPTER 13

CHAPTER 13

BREAK A SWEAT

USE THE WORKOUT PANTS

---

*It is exercise alone that supports the spirits, and
keeps the mind in vigor.*

—MARCUS TULLIUS CICERO

My first experience of exercise as a stress reliever was in high
school with extended neighborhood runs. Sure, some of
those workouts were motivated by the desire for a leaner look, but
they were also lifesavers amidst typical teenage dramas. I carried a
weighty leadership role during my junior and senior years as drum
major, conducting music for the marching, symphonic, and jazz
bands. My responsibilities created a great deal of strain for my still-
developing teenage brain, though. With weekend travel to compete
in different cities, statewide competitions each spring, and close
to fifteen band officers reporting to me, I hardly had a moment
to myself. The award-winning culture our school cultivated over

the decades was no joke—everyone had expectations. To add to the crazy, I also played trumpet in our citywide youth symphony year-round. Every waking moment not dedicated to studies was spent on music.

One particular day, in the middle of the stress, I felt like I just needed to run. Maybe it was the pressure of constant competitions, the weight of a rigorous practice schedule, or the general feeling of being overwhelmed, but for whatever reason, running seemed the only option. So I ran. No plan for where I was going or how far, I just needed movement, and in the exercise, I found release.

The release through running was new for me. From my earliest elementary memories, fitness looked like PE class, bike rides around our neighborhood, countless summers of swimming in our community pool, and a decade of shooting hoops in our driveway for fun. I never felt qualified or coordinated enough for team sports, and once I reached middle school, music took most of my time. But when I realized I could run, I kept running, and running and running (which I hope you heard in my best Forrest Gump voice).

In college, when I lived in dorms, I ran the "roller coaster"—a two-mile track of hills that would make any stomach turn. I established a rhythm that was doing far more than tightening my quads; it was helping me make sense of whatever I faced spiritually, emotionally, and relationally. The thrill of a sweat-drenched tank, mental clarity, and a tall glass of ice-cold water were the perfect payoff for the daily investment of time.

When I moved off campus for my last two years of college, my roommate ran cross-country on our college team. While I didn't have margin to pursue the official sport while working two jobs, she inspired me to go on longer runs. So I did. I ran a regular four-mile loop every morning in our town's historic district, then pushed myself toward an occasional thirteen-mile run. When I found my pace and cadence—what they call runner's high—I felt I could go on forever. Those long runs provided me with time to think and pray through issues and problems. You can solve a lot of problems during a half marathon!

The summer after my college graduation, I began to run trails. A couple of months in, I tripped on a tree root sticking out of the ground and twisted my knee. I walked the rest of the way home but didn't know it would be the beginning of a chronic ailment. Without health insurance coverage and with no money for surgery, I came to the realization that I'd have to heal on my own. My knee pain receded, but I found I could no longer run distances beyond 5k, or the pain would return.

I knew I couldn't let my exercise routine go. I picked up spin class in my twenties, weight training with a personal instructor, then yoga in my thirties. On my best weeks, I'd get in a rhythm: yoga, spin, weight-training classes, and always running or hiking outdoors. Working out in a gym is great, but nothing compares to exercising outdoors. The fresh air, salty sweat, and rush of endorphins brought a calming clarity, even in my most stressful seasons. That's why I maintain an exercise routine to this day, often outdoors.

GETTING GREEN WITH EXERCISE

I remember one particularly hard winter. I felt too cooped up in the gym, and I needed to get out in nature for some green exercise— the new term for activity in nature. Getting in green space, being near water, and breathing in fresh air are all proven elements to aid our mental health.[1] I knew this was true. But would I brave the elements in February and join the crazy runners on the Central Park loop?

Yes, I would, thank you.

GETTING IN GREEN SPACE, BEING NEAR WATER, AND BREATHING IN FRESH AIR ARE ALL PROVEN ELEMENTS TO AID OUR MENTAL HEALTH.

I'd barely run a hundred yards when I realized my eyes were brimming with tears. It was a release my body was begging for, but one I'd ignored. On that run, I came to understand that something releases during exercise. Whatever the body is storing, holding onto, must come out, and on that outdoor run, it did. I never got this same response inside a gym. Perhaps it was the beauty of creation or the solidarity that did it. I don't know. But I came to realize how an outdoor workout is a critical component of my exercise routine, and the more I considered this truth, the more I wondered: *Does this same truth apply to children?*

When our son Cade turned sixteen, the hormones kicked in, and he became extra moody. But due to the limited verbal vocabulary that accompanies his Down syndrome, he didn't have the words to vent his frustrations. I knew we needed to help Cade figure out how to express himself, express what he was feeling inside, and find his own form of release. He was born with exceptionally low muscle tone, even for a child with Down syndrome. He didn't walk until his third birthday and never had the endurance to run or the coordination for team sports. He's never had the core strength to balance on a typical bike, so getting Cade outdoors has always been a struggle, one which usually ends with him finding a place to sit under a shade tree.

Just like the rest of us, though, Cade's body was created to move, and I knew he needed to get outside for his mental health. So we did some investigating and found an incredible adult trike, the Mobo Triton.[2] With a low-to-the-ground frame and two back wheels, it allowed Cade to enjoy the outdoors, get a cardio workout, and take control of his own journey. After only a few days, Cade started asking to "ride bike" every day. It brought us so much joy to see his passion for exercise and his newfound independence. We knew Cade needed the same input we all do: the freedom to move, to exert himself, and then receive the benefits.

CREATING A RHYTHM OF EXERCISE

Science has long shown how exercise supports mental health by reducing anxiety and depression, and by improving self-esteem and cognitive function.[3] Without exercise, we become shells of ourselves, and ultimately, a lifetime without exercise leads to earlier death. Scientists indicate that preindustrial humans expended some 1000 kilocalories of activity per day, while modern humans average only 300 kilocalories.[4] What's the result of the lack of physical activity? It's been reported that there are 1.9 million deaths worldwide annually as a result of physical inactivity, roughly 1 in 25 of all deaths.[5] We have stopped sweating, and it's killing us.

You might think you aren't the jogging or "exercise type." I get it. But don't be intimidated. You don't have to go on a run or join a gym. The key is engaging a form of exercise that's challenging for *you*. Something that increases the heart rate and gets the blood, sweat, and positive emotions flowing. Even a short burst of ten minutes' brisk walking increases our mental alertness, energy, and positive mood.[6] Studies also show that just five minutes of outdoor activity—like hiking, jogging, or even outdoor yoga—can change mood and self-esteem.[7]

Remember, the exercise I'm advocating isn't just designed to help you fit into your favorite swimsuit or reduce your measurements in all the right places. For too long, the advertising and marketing around working out have been tied to looking good. It's true we get in better shape and build muscle tone, but it shouldn't be our primary motivation. Instead, we exercise to stay mentally and emotionally healthy. We exercise to increase our heart rate and stimulate the production of serotonin and dopamine, neurotransmitters God gave us to help us maintain our ideal state of well-being.

We've all heard that exercise—both indoor and outdoor—helps us offload stress. This isn't new information. But sometimes we lose sight of the most obvious practices when anxiety, panic, or depression hits. Instead of turning to the things God created to bring us some natural positive mojo, we look for comfort foods and self-soothing habits, nestled on a couch or hidden behind a screen, all of which are sedentary. All of which strip us of both internal and external strength.

AT SOME POINT, WE HAVE TO MAKE
A DECISION AND COMMIT.

At some point, we have to make a decision and commit. Some of us may even need to ask for help starting an exercise routine, and while it can sometimes be overwhelming to focus on a long-term exercise routine, remember: a routine is just a series of days strung together. So choose to make this day count. Don't end your day if you haven't moved your body in an intentional way. Whether it's a brisk sunset walk, a quick jog around the block, push-ups by your bedside before bedtime, or a couple of sets of jumping jacks, make sure to raise your heart rate for a period of time! Whatever you do, take action. God designed you to break a sweat. Your body, your brain, and your spirit will thank you for it.

⌐ REFLECTION QUESTIONS ⌐

1. DO YOU HAVE A REGULAR PRACTICE OF EXERCISE, ONE WHICH INVOLVES BREAKING A SWEAT A FEW TIMES A WEEK?

2. WHAT DISTRACTIONS DO YOU ALLOW TO HIJACK YOUR EXERCISE RHYTHMS?

3. IF YOU HAVEN'T EXERCISED IN A FEW MONTHS, GET OUTSIDE
   AND BREAK A SWEAT TODAY. WAIT THIRTY MINUTES, THEN
   ASK YOURSELF: HOW DO I FEEL? PHYSICALLY? EMOTIONALLY?
   MENTALLY?

PUSH YOURSELF

MOVE BEYOND YOUR COMFORT ZONE

CHAPTER 14

PUSH YOURSELF

MOVE BEYOND YOUR COMFORT ZONE

_To discover something truly great, one must set sail
and leave the shore of comfort._

—KHANG KIJARRO NGUYEN

There was too much chaos, too much stuff. Too many piles.

The truth was, the stacks had been building for years, but I'd
always found excuses to avoid them. I'd claim I didn't have enough
time to deal with all our stuff or that there were more important
responsibilities at hand. At best, I'd toss a few things and call it a day.
But all my excuses finally caught up with me. Every item needed
a place to call home.

It began with the simple practice of noticing. I noticed all the piles.
Piles in the laundry room. Piles on the kitchen island. Piles of

papers and office supplies stuffed in junk drawers, layered between random keys, loose change, and old cell phone chargers. I made my way to the bedroom, noticed the stacks of books by the bedside, the closet full of garments: formal wear, outerwear, and activewear I hadn't worn for years. Though my house wasn't dirty—dishes cleaned, floors vacuumed, and un-piled places dusted—the piles and stacks remained like survivors weathering a storm. I took note of our sprawl, our stacking, but how could I remedy the problem?

I'm sure this sounds silly to those of you who are natural organizers, who were Marie-Kondo-level organized before the guru of tidiness was a household name. But I find organization difficult. It's not my natural bent. To make matters worse, I so often stuff my schedule full of commitments that the last thing I want to do in my downtime is tend to the chronic chaos. But with new inspiration, I decided to attempt whatever it took to make sense of the mess. I determined to push myself to create a serene family space.

The art of organization is a learned skill, I knew that much. I read articles and watched online videos about how to declutter the house. I scoured Pinterest to find out how experts organized their closets, their shelves, their drawers and cabinets. I flipped through books about tidiness and decluttering, and formulated a plan.

I'd go through the piles room by room and create a place for everything in our home. I'd keep what I needed, donate or sell the things I didn't, and encourage Gabe and the kids to do the same. Every book, pen, pot, pan, and article of clothing found a permanent place, for when I finished with whatever I was using, it would go right back in its place. This was doable, I thought, even if these new parameters stretched the free spirit in me.

For weeks I pushed myself, until nearly everything had a home. (I say *nearly* because Gabe's closet became a bit of a dumping ground for the placeless things in our lives.) As the chaos of each room gave way to order, I noticed a sort of peace setting in, an immediate reward that kept me plowing ahead. In addition to peace, a sense of pride and accomplishment welled up. I could organize my life, even though it wasn't my natural inclination. I could learn new tricks, even in my early forties. In the wake of that sense of accomplishment, I leveled up. I bought organizational tools for my closet and little plastic trays with built-in dividers for the junk drawers in the kitchen. I got rid of things that wouldn't fit in those organizers or in my closet, and after months of work, the results were evident. My home was put together—and it was calm. So was my interior life. Pushing myself led to tangible, healthier results.

WHEN WE PUSH OURSELVES, WE DISCOVER HOW
MUCH WE CAN ACCOMPLISH, HOW BRAVE WE
CAN BE, AND HOW STRONG WE REALLY ARE.

In recent years, I've found unexpected joy in pushing myself, and not just organizationally. I've pushed myself in my writing life. I've pushed myself athletically, even picking up golf with Gabe. I've pushed myself as a mother as I've done the hard work of learning to connect with my children, learning how to listen to them and give them what they need as they grow into young adulthood. When we push ourselves, we discover how much we can accomplish, how brave we can be, and how strong we really are.

THE PAYOFF FOR PUSHING YOURSELF

New tasks present us with new obstacles, and when we overcome those obstacles we gain an increased sense of self-confidence. That confidence reminds us we can do most of the things we put our minds to, even if we're not the best at them. We can learn new skills, take on new hobbies, grow into opportunities, and connect with new people.

It's not all about personal growth, confidence-building, and connection, though. Pushing ourselves helps break the monotony of an otherwise mundane routine. Don't you get tired of making the same coffee, packing the same lunches, shopping for the same groceries, cleaning the same toilets, and paying the same bills? I know I do. Often, it's repetition that causes me to get a little bored, a little depressed. But when we break up the routine, when we try new things and create opportunities for different feelings to emerge, we grow, and we change the dynamic.

There are plenty of other reasons to push ourselves into the no-go zones we've set for ourselves. Embarking on new experiences that may feel awkward or uncomfortable brings with it a number of psychological benefits that help us develop a sense of pride and accomplishment and spur creativity. Perhaps most importantly, we feel engaged and happy, and we develop emotional resilience.[1] When we push ourselves, even in things we're already doing, we overcome fear of failure, an important emotional attribute in healthy individuals.

You might be asking, *What happens if I try something new, if I push myself and fail?* That's okay. Even when we fail, we learn new things.

We might learn different ways to attack a challenge or discover that an activity is not for us. These learning experiences add to our self-discovery, which in turns leads to growth. It's impossible to grow if we aren't okay failing. Any time we venture into new territory, any time we push ourselves, we are likely to experience setbacks. But when we push through, we find it's okay to try new things, no matter the outcome.

There are so many healthy rewards for challenging ourselves. Why wouldn't we do it?

THERE ARE SO MANY HEALTHY REWARDS FOR
CHALLENGING OURSELVES. WHY WOULDN'T WE DO IT?

So what might you do to push yourself? Could you try some new activity, some new physical endeavor like golf, or fly fishing, or even baking a cake? Could you take on a new hobby, a new craft, maybe learn a new language? Could you push yourself to learn a new song, run a faster mile, or fill an entire canvas? Could you learn to do something you've been putting off because it's outside your comfort zone, something like organizing your house? Push yourself and have fun with it, even if you don't think you can, aren't that talented, or don't know the lingo. See whether a little hard work and a little success, don't make a difference in your emotional and mental outlook.

↗ REFLECTION QUESTIONS ↖

1. ARE YOU THE KIND OF PERSON WHO ALWAYS PLAYS IT SAFE, OR ARE YOU THE SORT WHO WILL TAKE A RISK AND PUSH YOURSELF IN THAT TASK? EXPLAIN YOUR ANSWER.

2. WHEN IS THE LAST TIME YOU PUSHED YOURSELF INTO SOME NEW ENDEAVOR? DESCRIBE WHAT HAPPENED.

3. WHAT IS ONE WAY YOU CAN PUSH YOURSELF THIS WEEK, EVEN IN SOME ACTIVITY YOU'RE ALREADY DOING?

CONNECT

As you begin to experience the rewards of practicing the rhythms of rest and restoration, your heart, mind, and soul will come back to life. In that new life, you'll find you have something to offer the world around you.

The first two rhythms—Rest and Restore—are *input* rhythms, because they fill you back up. As your body and spirit experience renewal, you'll brim with energy. You'll discover new perspectives with an imagination awake to God's purposes in your life. With newfound confidence from a place of strength, you'll find deeper meaning and, more importantly, purpose in your everyday life.

Rest and restoration weren't designed to help us self-actualize or achieve some higher state of consciousness. God has bigger, and less selfish, plans than that. Our peace is meant to thrust us forward into a life of meaning and purpose with those around us. That's why I call the next two rhythms—Connect and Create—*output* rhythms, rhythms that help us reach out to bless and help others. After all, being filled up isn't just for your benefit, but for the benefit of those around you. Spiritual community and cultural renewal can only happen when we look outside ourselves and engage with others from a full heart.

As we establish rhythms of Rest and Restoration, we automatically move to the output rhythm of Connection. We can't help it. Once we've got something to offer, we're ready to give it away. The power of relationship is a healing balm unlike any other rhythm in my life. In my worst moments, the unexpected phone call from a friend, the last-minute meet-up for an acaí bowl (the way to my heart), time with friends, or the fun of family brings peace and purpose like little else. But if we aren't careful, in our hurried lives, connection can slip through the cracks. And if it does, we might forego invitations to even deeper healing.

We were created for connection, and when we are closely knit within our community, we are at our best, flourishing and full of life. But in our cultural moment, this takes work, planning, courage, and commitment.

WE WERE CREATED FOR CONNECTION, AND WHEN WE ARE CLOSELY KNIT WITHIN OUR COMMUNITY, WE ARE AT OUR BEST, FLOURISHING AND FULL OF LIFE.

In this section, we'll share rhythms of connection that lead us out of isolation and into healing connection. As we explore these rhythms, ask yourself: *Do I have meaningful connections in my life, connections that help me maintain spiritual and mental health, or am I sinking deeper into the stress and anxiety of isolation?* Be honest. Take notes. If you feel the need to reach out to a friend at any point along the way, don't wait. Find someone to come alongside you as you explore the power of connection.

BE THE
FRIEND
YOU
WISH TO
HAVE

INITIATE FRIENDSHIP

CHAPTER 15

BE THE FRIEND YOU WISH TO HAVE

INITIATE FRIENDSHIP

---

*Perfect friendship is the friendship of those who are
alike in virtue, for these individuals wish well to each
other in all circumstances and thus these friendships
are good in themselves.*

—ARISTOTLE

As we arrived at our new home, shiny keys in hand, Gabe told
me to prepare myself. He was carrying me over the threshold.
As we pulled into the driveway, the movers were busy hustling
furniture and boxes into the house, and we watched as they moved
the brief history of our adulthood, which had been boxed up and
dragged all over the Eastern Seaboard, into our home. After living
in apartments for several years and getting used to the transient lifestyle, we were putting down roots in Tennessee. As we approached

the front steps, I noticed a large bag hanging from the front door and couldn't help but wonder what someone had left. Was this our first housewarming gift?

Before Gabe could hoist me into his arms, I jogged to the door to peek inside the bag. There were hundreds of colorful bows of all shapes and sizes, and they filled the space. I stuck my hand down through the rainbows of color to see what was there—nothing but bows. I opened the note attached to the outside of the package and read: "Put these bows on all of your moving boxes and tell your kids it's Christmas. It makes unpacking way more fun! Love you, Elisabeth." It was just a little note, but a warm reminder that three years in, Nashville had become home. Forging friendships in a new community takes time, and it isn't always easy.

Just a couple of years prior, I had awakened to the realization that I was lonely and disconnected. I was so disconnected, in fact, that I wondered, *If I moved away today, would anyone notice?* At the age of forty, rebuilding community and deep friendships was a different ballgame than it had been in my twenties. Everyone was busy and saddled with the responsibilities that come with careers and kids. What's more, they had plenty of time-honored friendships and weren't looking to add more cookouts, birthday parties, or dinner dates to the calendar.

It wasn't just them, though. I played no small part. On many weekends my work took me out of town, so I missed out on social gatherings at home. I missed supper clubs and church events, all the places where new friendship could be forged. Though I met incredible people and even made a few new friends, I chose to keep things shallow, wondering how I could invest if I was always moving, always without margin.

I knew the importance of friendship in my life. Since adolescence, God has blessed me with close friends. In high school I was one of a handful of girls who stuck together like glue. Then, in college, there was another crew of us who went through a weekly Bible study together over four years. We shared Scriptures and secrets, and eventually stood up in each other's weddings. In my twenties, new women came into my life, and we grew close, held each other's babies, brought each other meals, hosted playdates and birthday parties. We were open and honest with each other, and that atmosphere of openness and honesty gave us a sense of belonging and love.

Gabe and I were in our thirties when we moved to New York City, and starting over in a new town wasn't easy. But in his faithfulness, God brought me a new group of friends, and we grew close. Over Tuesday morning coffee on the Upper West Side and Monday night Bible study in Brooklyn, hearts were bonded. When I reflect on how rich those groups were, how honest and lasting, how they helped me adjust to a new season, I'm so grateful.

There was another side to friendship, too, though. Over the years, I learned how fickle friends can be and how anxious that fickleness makes me. I had two friends who bailed in hard seasons: one in my twenties, one in my thirties. At the time, I couldn't fathom losing either of them. So each time, I became the squeaky wheel that demanded their attention. I worked harder to earn their love, tried to change who I was to convince them to stick around. It didn't work, and both times I was left wondering, *What is wrong with me?*

AM I TOO MUCH OR NOT ENOUGH? WHY DO I PLACE SO MUCH PRESSURE ON FRIENDSHIPS?

This anxiety bled into my other relationships. If a friend commented that I was too vulnerable, I would rein it in. Too serious, I'd lighten up. Too passionate, I'd get silly. I'd change anything so as not to lose another friend. It hurts too much. Dancing on eggshells, I was afraid to be myself, afraid to live into the fullness of who God created me to be. But no matter how I tried to please people or change so they'd accept me, I couldn't shake the anxiety.

Am I too much or not enough? Why do I place so much pressure on friendships?

Then, the critique of a few friends became too loud, and before I knew it, a transfer occurred. The lies I heard stopped coming from them and began coming from my own thoughts. I was listening to the voice in my head more often than I was trusting the heart God gave me.

Do I even know how to pick the right friends?

Am I placing the gift of friends over the God who gives them?

I'd let a few bad experiences reshape my outlook, and I needed a shift.

Hoping to change my attitude, which wasn't getting me anywhere, I started studying friendship. I discovered that, centuries ago, Aristotle defined three different types of friends who tend to make their way into our lives. There are friendships based on *utility*, friendships based on *pleasure*, and friendships based on *virtue*—the ideal. These friendships go deeper than convenience and encourage us in our shared commitments.[1]

Aristotle wrote, "Those who love because of utility love because of what is good for themselves, and those who love because of pleasure do so because of what is pleasant to themselves."[2] Yet what one finds useful or pleasurable, Aristotle wrote, "is not permanent but is always changing; thus, when the reason for the friendship is done away, the friendship is dissolved."[3] This rang true. A few of the deep friendship hurts I'd experienced fit those first two categories. Life seasons had brought us together, but shared passions and commitments weren't always in the mix. I'd been just as guilty of being a friend of convenience, rather than a friend of virtue, as anyone.

Where have I only wanted to be a friend of utility or pleasure?

As I read Aristotle, I knew I needed to rededicate myself to making friends with people with whom I shared commitments. But where would I start?

One day I called a long-distance friend of twenty years, Trina, and I shared how tired I felt at the thought of making new friends. She's known me since I started my grown-up life, before babies and toddlers and teens, and she's stuck with me through all my highs and lows. After I spilled my guts, she reminded me how capable I'd been in faithful friendship, especially when I felt free to be myself. I'd experienced the truth of Aristotle's musings: I found it easy to sacrifice for friends who were like-minded and shared a similar vision for life. Trina convinced me it was all worth risking again and reminded me of an axiom she lives by: Be the friend you wish to have.

———

BE THE FRIEND YOU WISH TO HAVE.

———

It's that simple. With a hue of "golden rule" about it, this adage reminded me that if I could love my neighbor and friends as much as I love myself, my friendships would be remarkable. I knew that remarkable friends alleviate the stress of superficial friendships and the anxiety that so often comes with loneliness, but to make these kinds of friends, I'd need to be a consistent friend myself. If I wanted a trusted circle, I'd need to be trustworthy myself. If I wanted an authentic friend, I'd need to be authentic myself.

I decided to make some changes. I'd let down the walls and look for opportunities to connect more with those around me. I'd be open to whomever God brought my way while I adjusted my rhythms to make space for what he might have in mind.

I began taking fewer engagements so I could stay home more. I created more margin in my calendar so I could be available when needed, not just when I could squeeze it in. I stopped adjusting who I am in order to satisfy others, and I became more confident in the ways God has designed me for relationship. I did my best to live intentionally and with vulnerability, moving into relationships with like-minded people.

I set out to live in this new way: *being the friend I wanted to have.* As I did, I found I was cultivating deep friendships, friendships that were covered with grace, friendships that were easy. The anxiety I'd carried about making new connections disappeared, and I looked forward to spending time with my new friends. When I stopped focusing on myself, when I focused on how I could love friends well, encourage them, and show up for their most important moments and needs, everything changed.

REIMAGINING FRIENDSHIP

What if we let God be in charge of our friendships? What if we trusted that he places the right people in our lives at the right times? What if we were authentic with those people, letting them see the good, the bad, and the uncertain? What if we sacrificed, showed up for those people, and were generous, gracious, and forgiving? And in the difficult seasons when friends think we're too much, or not enough, or need to change, what if we let them walk away? (That'd be freeing, wouldn't it?)

I don't always do this well, of course. Sometimes I still give conditionally. I still get my feelings hurt, still nurse my hurt, and sometimes I still try to become what I think my friends want me to be. (Old habits die hard.) But I'm learning, and the more I return to the idea of being the kind of friend I'd wish to have, the easier it is to right the ship and live the life of friendship God intends for me, to have friendships that keep me showing up.

We show up for each other in the little ways when we practice presence, proximity, and permanence. When we're authentic. When we bless. When we love. As we push into this kind of friendship, we find a rhythm of connection that rescues us from the anxiety of performance-based friendships and seats us in a community of love. It's this community of love that gives us the courage to go out into the world as the blessing we were made to be.

BE A FRIEND, BE A BLESSING

My friend Amber has a unique way of sharing the blessing of friendship in her own community. Year after year, she and a group of friends gather for birthday celebrations, and when they do, they go around the table, each giving the birthday girl or boy a blessing for the upcoming year. Moved by the story, wishing to be the same kind of friend to her, I left her a voicemail of blessing on her birthday saying:

> I've watched a peace settle over you this past year, as you carry a quiet confidence that God is with you and guiding your steps. No matter what others think, God knows your heart is diligent and willing and humble. I've been blessed in your friendship over the years, but this year in particular I'm grateful for a friend who is steadfast in her faith and loyal to her people. Thanks for pulling me in, even across the miles. I count your friendship a joy because you're approachable, relatable, easy to confide in, and grace-filled. I can't wait to see how this overflow blesses the next year.

It was a simple thing, really, but even as I shared the blessing with Amber, I felt the truth of Trina's words washing over me. I was being the friend I wished to have, the kind of friend Amber is to me. In that moment, I felt joy and peace. In that moment, there was no anxiety.

Do you have difficulty making friends? Do you lack meaningful connection in your life? Are your friendships shallow? Are they based in utility or exchange or convenience? Reach out. Be intentional. Be the friend you wish to have. See if it doesn't cultivate the kind of friendships you want, friendships of love, blessing, mutual support, and freedom.

⌖ REFLECTION QUESTIONS ⌖

1. DO YOU FEEL ANXIETY, STRESS, OR PRESSURE WHEN YOU THINK ABOUT FRIENDSHIPS? WHY?

2. DO YOU HAVE A GROUP OF FRIENDS YOU CAN LAUGH, CRY, AND SHARE EVEN YOUR DARKEST OR SADDEST MOMENTS WITH? IF NOT, WHAT ARE THE BARRIERS TO THAT KIND OF FRIENDSHIP?

3. WHAT ARE THE QUALITIES OF YOUR IDEAL FRIEND? HOW COULD YOU BE THIS FRIEND TO ANOTHER?

LEAD WITH VULNERABILITY

BETTER TOGETHER

CHAPTER 16

CHAPTER 16

LEAD WITH VULNERABILITY

BETTER TOGETHER

---

*Authenticity is a collection of choices that we have to
make every day. It's about the choice to show up and
be real. The choice to be honest. The choice to let our
true selves be seen.*

—BRENÉ BROWN

A few months back I met some friends for impromptu burgers
and fries, and in my attempt to let off some steam, I shared a
bit more intimately than was appropriate for this particular group
setting. I immediately wanted to take back my last couple of sen-
tences, but there they were, hanging out there, for everyone to take
in. One person began to press further, and with each subsequent
question, I grew more and more awkward in front of the group. My
attempt to confide, to expose some of my current tensions and fears,
went sideways. Finally someone saved me by changing the subject.

I scurried to the bathroom, then took care of the check. I couldn't get to my car fast enough.

I learned something important about vulnerability that day. I learned to be thoughtful about *what* to share, *when* to share, and *with whom* to share. Group settings aren't always the best places for vulnerable conversations that require more explanation. You can risk being misunderstood at best, judged at worst.

As you develop your own trusted circle, exercise wisdom regarding when, where, and with whom you'll share the deeper things. When you find the right people, keep revealing your deepest self with them. After all, while vulnerability with the wrong sorts of folks fosters feelings of inferiority and judgment, vulnerability with the right people brings trust, bolsters our feelings of love, and brings hope.

As the beloved social worker Brené Brown writes, "Vulnerability is the birthplace of love, belonging, joy, courage, empathy, and creativity. It is the source of hope, empathy, accountability, and authenticity. If we want greater clarity in our purpose or deeper and more meaningful spiritual lives, vulnerability is the path."[1]

THE CONNECTING POWER OF VULNERABILITY

Gabe was the first to teach me the connecting power of vulnerability. For twenty-three years he's seen my absolute worst yet believed in my absolute best. He never demands I be less raw or less real, and he's always been tender with my heart. He has provided a safe place for me to be vulnerable, to confess and share everything. In that vulnerability, he has been patient with my healing. He has pointed me back to the rescue of Jesus. He has been there for me in ways the crowd never could be, in ways the crowd never would if they could see my darkest days, and as he's created space for me to be vulnerable, I've found freedom from guilt and shame. I've found healing.

While Gabe was my first guide on my journey toward vulnerability, my friend Lauren has taught me how to understand vulnerability in relationships outside of my marriage. A few years ago, we became fast friends upon our simultaneous moves to Franklin from different cities. From the beginning, I knew I could tell her anything without judgment. She's helped me appreciate the freedom and safety vulnerability brings when entrusted to the right people. We've shared tears, laughter, and loads of prayer. She's been a godsend.

One autumn, Lauren and I spent a girls' weekend away at the beach, to relax, play, and recalibrate. The first sunny afternoon, we went for a walk along the gulf and within minutes, I began to unload things I didn't realize needed to get out. Sometimes we need the right setting and the right person to uncover the wounds that have burdened our hearts, and that's exactly what took place. She listened, shared her own struggles, was empathetic, and offered some well-placed advice. Our afternoon talk turned toward prayer and impromptu counseling with her wise mama, who also happened to be in town. I'd revealed some of my deepest heartaches to a trusted friend, and she responded in kind. By the end of the day, I felt more connected, more known. And when the weekend was over, I went back home freer, more secure, and healthier than I'd been in a while. This is the power of being vulnerable with someone who loves and cares.

Jeff Polzer, a professor of organizational behavior at Harvard, says, "People tend to think of vulnerability in a touchy-feely way, but that's not what's happening. It's about sending a really clear signal that you have weaknesses, that you could use help."[2] He developed a vulnerability loop model that displays how connection and trust can happen quickly between two individuals: Person A sends a signal of vulnerability, Person B detects this signal, Person B responds by signaling their own vulnerability, Person A detects this signal, and finally, a norm is established; closeness and trust increase.[3]

The key to deep connection is found in our ability to detect the signal and respond with our own vulnerability. It's not enough to simply listen; we must respond. We have to be willing, as John Townsend says, "to get down in the well with someone"[4] and see life from their point of view. If at first this sounds risky and hard to imagine, stay with me. Taking small steps, choosing to trust, and being vulnerable with the right people can bring a freedom and connection like you've never known.

Lauren is one of a handful of girlfriends who have taught me the power of vulnerability. Some I've known since high school, while others I met in my twenties. From family potluck nights when we shared the same town to walking through the great pain of unexpected loss, these women have shown me the deep power of connection. I've enjoyed more girlfriend getaways over the years than I can count—always making it a priority to spend time together face-to-face as much as possible. When we get together, our time consists of life updates through laughter and tears, creative gift-giving, incredible food, and midnight pajama conversations that won't quit.

These friends have helped me when I needed comfort and challenged me when I needed confrontation. When I opened up about my anxiety and panic years ago, they met me in my most vulnerable place and helped me believe wholeness was possible. We've shared a lot with each other through the years. And though the text thread topics have moved on from toddler life to our newbie teen drivers having fender benders and which essential oil to put on a neck rash, we are committed to showing up.

The thing that has kept me close to each of these women is their willingness to be vulnerable. There's a safety in walking through highs and lows over the years, in giving and receiving grace. While we've lived a good part of our lives in different cities, it feels like we are growing old together. From new mamas who stood by each other in labor and delivery rooms, to toddler playdates, to juggling the tween angst of middle school, to caring for aging parents and walking through tender marriages, we've stuck by each other through it all.

In so many ways, Gabe, Lauren, and these other incredible women have reflected to me what God's love looks and feels like over the long haul. God knows my worst but believes my best. He invites me to share vulnerably with him, to lay it all bare, and as I do, he reveals more of his perfect father-heart. He becomes my safe place, my refuge. He frees me from the opinions of others and the worries of my own heart. He shows me how to receive abundantly so I can serve others, not out of my strength but his. He teaches me how to make space for the vulnerability of others, too.

TAKE THE RISK AND FIND CONNECTION

Let's face it: we all need to feel this type of connection, attachment, and love. It must move from being an idea to becoming a tangible part of our lives. When we experience deep connection, we are healthier, more confident, more known. These women and our rhythms of connection have played a significant part in my story. Because of the trust and bearing of one another's burdens, we've each become stronger. But this isn't always the case. Allow me to share a word of caution about vulnerability. Sometimes it backfires.

Perhaps you've tried to share your heart with a trusted friend, parent, or spouse, and somewhere along the way you were shamed for those feelings. Instead of being met in your vulnerability, instead of being held, cherished, and understood, you felt the sting of betrayal. Instead of experiencing the vulnerability loop, you experienced a vulnerability block. I know this pain, and I've listened to countless stories of others who have, too. But that doesn't mean we should stop being vulnerable.

The enemy of our souls wants us to be isolated and alone. He knows that when we're isolated, we're easy prey. Why? When we're alone and vulnerable, we feel afraid. When we're together and vulnerable, we become brave. A brave group of vulnerable people acting together in faith is not easily overcome by anxiety and stress.

Where might you need to be vulnerable in this season? Perhaps a struggle with insecurity? Comparison? A relationship you're longing to see restored? It's hard to know where to begin unless we take a moment to pause and reflect, to give language to what we've been internalizing. We cannot share things about ourselves we don't yet realize. But once we become aware, we can open up to others.

With whom can you share your deepest thoughts? Is it with your spouse, your child, your parents, a friend? Pick up the phone and make a call. Connect—really connect in true vulnerability—with those you love. Your courage to bring your whole, beautiful self out into the open just might inspire them to do the same. In that vulnerable connection, you'll bolster each other's courage, give each other love, and point each other to God, who can strengthen you even in the darkest hour.

↗ REFLECTION QUESTIONS ↖

1. JOURNAL ABOUT THE LAST TIME YOU SHARED VULNERABLY WITH ANOTHER PERSON. HOW DID YOU FEEL AFTER YOU SHARED?

2. WHAT ARE THE THINGS THAT KEEP YOU FROM BEING VULNERABLE WITH OTHERS?

3. WHAT IS THE ONE THING YOU'D RATHER NOT SHARE WITH ANYONE, THE THING THAT, IF YOU SHARED IT, WOULD BRING YOU FREEDOM? WHO COULD YOU SHARE IT WITH?

OPEN-PORCH POLICY

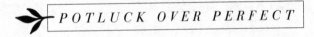

POTLUCK OVER PERFECT

CHAPTER 17

OPEN-PORCH POLICY

POTLUCK OVER PERFECT

The primary impulse of hospitality is to create a safe and welcoming place where a stranger can be converted into a friend.

—JOSHUA W. JIP

C ome on over, and bring the whole family; we can't wait to see you!" These are words I never tire of hearing. The welcome of friends who feel like family welcoming me in, no matter the season, time of night, or need—it offers a relief that is rare in our world.

My cousins, the Scarberry family, are lifelong teachers of this kind of open-door hospitality. Hospitality is in their blood; I suppose they come by it honestly. Going all the way back to my childhood, every memory I have of visiting their family—usually after a twenty-two-hour drive from Florida to their Wisconsin home—is full of warmth and welcome. There we'd be pummeled with laughter and given frequent bear hugs. My Uncle Rick and Aunt Martha spoiled us rotten, Martha filling our bellies with meals made from her signature recipes. They lived with an infectious spirit of generosity that they passed down to the next generation.

Today their fortysomething-year-old children carry on their legacy. But my cousins' commitment to a life of togetherness didn't come without intention. Eighteen years ago, my Uncle Rick (their daddy) passed away from a heart attack. Nine years after that, my aunt was diagnosed with pancreatic cancer. She passed away several months later. Still, their legacy of loving each other through hospitality remained strong.

These days, all three brothers and their families live in south Florida. They moved from all over the country to the same neighborhood. Their sister lives a couple hours away and visits often for one reason: being in close proximity to one another helped them structure their lives for deepened relationship and family connection. The priority of being together was more important than their individual opportunities, their careers, and their monetary successes.

In a culture that praises the individual spirit—to go and be and do whatever you want, wherever you want—I admire how they've prioritized connection over ambition. What's more, they continue to invite others into their family life. They remain a hospitable people who invite new friends to share in their home cooking and impromptu evening get-togethers, who have wide-open households, are a breath of fresh air in a closed-door culture.

Our family has benefitted from the Scarberrys' open-door attitude. Whether it's New Year's Eve, Easter, or midsummer, if we're in the vicinity, we're welcomed in, and it's an invitation we'd be crazy not to accept. Every holiday their home is packed to the gills, the kitchen island loaded with meals on rotation. There's chocolate gravy and homemade biscuits for breakfast, slow-roasted pork shoulder for lunch, homemade pizzas for dinner. Kids work up appetites between meals, running from house to house, riding bikes in the neighborhood, swimming in the community pool, and dancing to karaoke until midnight. There never seems to be a limit to the number of people my cousins can host in their homes. There are always new babies, new recipes, and conversations about life changes. We share everything together, even the epic influenza virus of 2017 when all forty of us wound up ringing in the New Year by kneeling to the porcelain god day and night.

Families like the Scarberrys are the epitome of fun. They are comfortable removing all barriers. They believe *more* is better, and *now* is just as good as tomorrow. Instead of hiding away in comfort or isolation, they share their abundance and remind me how the true power of connection takes place when we welcome others into our lives and spaces. I don't know about you, but this is the kind of family I want to have.

AN OPEN-PORCH POLICY

Gabe and I continue to be inspired by this open-door policy, so when we saw our home in Franklin for the first time, we knew it'd be a perfect fit for our family. It had a long, wide front porch, and we could envision it lined with rockers. I imagined then what our home would come to be: a place for family and friends to gather.

From the first blooms of spring to the final leaves of autumn, we get full use out of this porch. On the occasional morning, I'll watch the sunrise with Gabe, coffee in hand. Sometimes our favorite cardinal will perch on a rocker adjacent to us, constantly flying into his reflection in the window, wondering if he's welcome. He is. I've found the calm of the country, and I want to offer that same place of peace to anyone who might be craving it, even when we are not home.

So we expanded our open-door policy, developing an open-porch policy. When someone needs to exhale, clear their head, or dream, they are always welcome. Recently, I found myself running through an airport between flights and got a text asking if I was home. A friend wanted to come by and just catch a breath. Even though I was not at home, the answer was an immediate, "Please come."

We've hosted board meetings and impromptu birthday parties on our porch, watched firefly-catching on summer evenings at dusk, and shared lemonade with friends traveling through town. Just the other day, our friend Tim set up a painting station from our porch steps, a tin of watercolors in hand. I've prayed with friends on our rocking chairs as they were preparing to move to a new city, cried tears as my mother-in-law shared her journey of becoming cancer-free, and reflected on fond moments with my sister as we processed the death of our dad. When the cold creeps in, we move the fellowship indoors. Whether it's afternoon cookie decorating with teen girls, an impromptu coffee or brunch, or a festive "friendsgiving potluck," everyone huddles around the kitchen island, eager to connect.

CREATING A SUSTAINABLE CULTURE OF HOSPITALITY
REQUIRES CASUAL FREQUENCY, GETTING TOGETHER
OFTEN, COMING AS YOU ARE, HOSTING AS YOU ARE.

Hospitality doesn't require an elaborate meal with your best china or making sure every nook and cranny is clean. People crave connection and love to gather, even if the house isn't perfectly put together. Creating a sustainable culture of hospitality requires casual frequency, getting together often, coming as you are, hosting as you are. Embracing connection over perfection lifts my spirits and encourages the hearts of my friends.

A year ago I wanted to establish new holiday traditions and connect some incredible women across our city. Our house wasn't put together, though. We still had a construction project hanging over our heads, and our yard was a mess. With all my obligations, I found it difficult to keep a clean house. But I pushed those worries aside and, on a whim, texted twenty friends who didn't know one another and invited them to a Friday morning Christmas brunch. It was a chance to introduce people who needed to know one another but would likely never meet without a little intention. I was surprised when eighteen said they could come! Then, twenty-four hours prior, a woman on the thread suggested we make our little gathering an ugly-sweater brunch. By nine o'clock the next morning, half the group had rummaged through their kids' closets or run by a thrift store, throwing on any tacky sweater they could find.

This impromptu hilarity forged an immediate bond. As each guest arrived, laughter erupted among the women, who were complete strangers but becoming fast friends. Now, a year later, this "Christmas Brunch at Rebekah's" group text thread is still going strong! In the past twelve months, we've had birth updates, adoption updates, Haiti updates, moving updates, heart surgery and pediatric intensive care unit updates.

BRINGING THE OUTSIDER IN

Maybe you practice this kind of hospitality, but it's a dying virtue in our culture, even though it's needed now more than ever. A recent Pew Research Center study shows that among US-born adults who have lived in more than one community, nearly four in ten (38 percent) say the place they consider home isn't where they're living now,[1] and with only a third of Americans knowing their neighbors, we're all a lot lonelier than we used to be.[2] Not only that, but with our presence becoming more digitized and less embodied, our methods of communication don't feed something we need—*proximate human connection*. In a polarized climate, where people feel more divided than ever, where they're incentivized to huddle up with those who think, look, and believe like they do, we have an opportunity to do the opposite—to welcome people in.

Jon Tyson, our pastor from New York, says, "Biblical hospitality is an environment of welcome where a person's identity goes from an outsider to an insider so they can belong. It's turning the other into 'one another.'" Isn't that what we all crave? Shifting from being *the other* to becoming *one another*? The older I get, the more I'm paring down what matters most to my heart for the second half of life. I want to make it my mission to help people belong. I want our home to welcome not just our nuclear family, but anyone God puts in front of us, whether it's a child abandoned on the other side of the world or a local college student or a gathering of the ugly-sweater club.

WHEN I OPEN MY HOME, WHEN I CONNECT
WITH OTHERS BY EXTENDING HOSPITALITY, I LIVE
INTO THE GENEROSITY OF GOD'S DESIGN.

When I open my home, when I connect with others by extending hospitality, I live into the generosity of God's design. Pressure and stress melt away as I share space with others. Through hospitality, I find true community, connection with friends, family, and those we now love or soon will because I made myself available and opened our doors.

⌐ REFLECTION QUESTIONS ⌐

1. WHO IS THE MOST HOSPITABLE PERSON YOU KNOW? WHAT CHARACTERISTICS OF HOSPITALITY DO THEY EXUDE?

2. WHEN WAS THE LAST TIME YOU OPENED YOUR HOME TO FRIENDS OR FAMILY?

3. HOW MIGHT YOU EXTEND HOSPITALITY TO SOMEONE THIS MONTH?

BEAR EACH OTHER'S BURDENS

CARRY THE LOAD

CHAPTER 18

BEAR EACH OTHER'S BURDENS

CARRY THE LOAD

Bear one another's burdens.

—THE APOSTLE PAUL

O ur family anticipated my father's passing, and we spent his final week taking turns at his bedside, singing psalms and hymns while he nodded wide-eyed to each reading of Scripture. I shared with Dad what was about to happen, how he'd soon be with Jesus. The veil was so thin; his countenance glowed. He knew, I knew, we all knew: the end was near.

Dad took his final breath in the early morning hours of a Tuesday. When I woke to the finality of the news, I wept in my bed. At dusk, Gabe, my sister, the kids, and I huddled around the living room as family, sharing every memory of Dad we could remember—all the stories I didn't want my children to forget.

The next day I dropped my sister off at the airport and merged onto the interstate for the long drive home. It was the first time in three weeks I'd been alone. There was a torrential downpour, rain washing a layer of pollen off my car, the buildings, and the streets, and when the clouds cracked open, so did my heart, releasing sobs to match the torrent against my windshield. The car crawled as I struggled to see through my tears, finally alone and therefore able to release the weight. I was free from the expectations of others, from eyes shifting in concern, from phrases like "Thank you so much for dropping in," and "I'm so grateful for your prayers." I'd pumped out these phrases on repeat for days.

As I drove, I recalled an ancient mourning tradition I'd read about. In Roman times, after the passing of a loved one, women stored their tears in a bottle. It was a sign of respect to the person who passed, and the more tears that were collected, the more valuable the bottle became.[1] This tradition reminded me of the story from Scripture of the woman who crashed the wedding party, who lost herself in a debt of gratitude when she encountered Jesus. She fell to her knees and tears poured from her, falling all over his feet. Jesus was moved by this sacred outpouring of heartbreak, her gift of vulnerability. He praised her for it, blessed her, even said, "Your sins are forgiven."[2] Her tears were the pathway to her healing.

———

CRYING CAN BE OUR BODY'S NATURAL WAY
TO OFFLOAD STRESS AND ANXIETY, TO PUSH
INTO NEW SEASONS OF HEALING.

———

I've never thought of tears as cleansing, but as I drove, I knew that's what they were. My tears were somehow purifying my heart, washing out so much grief and pain. As I cried, it was as if my tears, too, were spilling onto Jesus' feet. I could almost feel the beginnings of healing setting in.

My counselor has a catchphrase: "If you're crying, you're healing." It's a truth counselors, pastors, priests, spiritual advisors, and folks with high emotional intelligence have known for years, and research backs up this notion. When we allow ourselves to feel, to release, it has positive effects on our emotional state. Crying can be self-soothing and elevate mood better than any antidepressant.[3] "Crying does not only mentally cleanse us, it can cleanse our body, too. Tears produced by stress help the body get rid of chemicals that raise cortisol, the stress hormone."[4] Crying can be our body's natural way to offload stress and anxiety, to push into new seasons of healing.

MADE TO PROCESS OUR PAIN WITH OTHERS

The rain and tears provided immediate relief that day, but tears shed in solitude won't ever cure our grief. Waves of depression came knocking for the next two months. Though it had been six years since my last undoing, I was still familiar with this visitor. It takes on the shape of the fetal position in my closet. One month after my daddy's death, on my forty-fourth birthday, there I was again, slumped down against the floor, hiding behind coats and boots.

My heart was hemorrhaging, and I couldn't seem to find stability through the tears. A good friend, Bob, called me to check in. He wanted to see how I was processing this significant loss. He must have sensed the loop of grief, must have known I was spinning out of control. I told him I didn't want to spiral into more panic and anxiety as a result of not processing my grief well. I was having a hard time knowing how to walk through it all. He listened and listened, and when I finished, he spoke plainly. "Be careful who you give the microphone in your life," he said. "There will be voices out there, but only a few have earned the right to be on high volume. Only a few will be real life-givers in this time of grief."

I listened to Bob—he'd earned the right to speak into my life—and when we hung up, I reached out to others who'd been with me through the dark times, who'd helped me pull through. I didn't have to process this pain alone, I could walk through the journey of grief with others. I reached out to my community for impromptu prayer walks, acaí bowl confessions, front porch rocking chair drop-ins, and Marco Polo chats with dear ones from afar. I shared my grief, my tears, and some of the better memories of my dad with these loved ones.

Through our consistent time together, I began to pull out of my own pain, and on occasion, the roles shifted. While they might not have just lost their dad, my closest friends were still walking through their own hard things. As I shared my burden with them, I invited them to share theirs with me. How were they doing? What were they facing? How could I encourage their hearts while nurturing mine? We were made to process our pain and sadness with one another.

As we bore each other's burdens in real time, I pulled out of my own darkness. Day by day, week by week, month by month, intentionally holding friends close, I felt connected while facing the grief of losing my dad.

MEANINGFUL CONNECTION HELPS
US OVERCOME GRIEF

We weren't designed to beat our fears, our anxieties, and our worries on our own. We weren't meant for isolation. We were meant to encourage one another in darker seasons, to be the church of healing to one another. Paul said as much in his letter to the Galatians, writing, "Share each other's burdens, and in this way obey the law of Christ."[5]

> WE WEREN'T DESIGNED TO BEAT OUR FEARS, OUR
> ANXIETIES, AND OUR WORRIES ON OUR OWN.

Meaningful connections with others help us overcome grief, depression, and sorrow. As Dr. Frank McAndrew wrote, "Humans are hardwired to interact with others, especially during times of stress. When we go through a trying ordeal alone, a lack of emotional support and friendship can increase our anxiety and hinder our coping ability."[6] But with emotional support, our bodies respond in kind. As Emily Sohn wrote for the *Washington Post*, "Plenty of studies have revealed biological theories that may explain what makes us healthier when we feel supported: lower blood pressure, better hormone function, stronger immune systems and possibly lower levels of inflammation."[7]

Once we receive and respond, once we find healing, it's our turn to bear the burdens of others. Together, we find that the burdens of life are somehow bearable, and we find the confidence and strength to overcome.

Do you have burdens you've carried in silence? Have you held back tears, refused to carry them to God and to others? If so, you may be robbing yourself of a key point of connection, a point of connection that might just renew your soul.

⟶ REFLECTION QUESTIONS ⟵

1. WHEN IS THE LAST TIME YOU CRIED TEARS OF SORROW?

2. WHEN IS THE LAST TIME YOU SHARED YOUR SORROW WITH OTHERS?

3. THINK OF THE PEOPLE IN YOUR LIFE. WHO HAS A BURDEN YOU CAN HELP SHOULDER? WRITE THEIR NAME DOWN AND COMMIT TO REACHING OUT TO THEM THIS WEEK.

HUGS ALL
AROUND

THE POWER OF PHYSICAL TOUCH

CHAPTER 19

HUGS ALL AROUND

THE POWER OF PHYSICAL TOUCH

*When we honestly ask ourselves which person in
our lives means the most to us, we often find that
it is those who, instead of giving advice, solutions,
or cures, have chosen rather to share our pain and
touch our wounds with a warm and tender hand.*

—HENRI NOUWEN

Riding the subway in New York was not my favorite experience. Thanks to my earlier years of panic attacks and my
tendency to feel trapped underground, heading onto the escalator
was never fun. But it was always a bit more entertaining if my teen
son could go with me. Cade experiences life in a different light.
He sees the world through a rose-tinted Down syndrome lens. He's
never met a stranger, and if someone seems a little out of sorts, his
remedy is a good, old-fashioned hug.

But in Manhattan, Cade operated at a deficit. The playing field was not always equal. The city rewards speed, efficiency, high production, and performance. People don't have time for needless chitchat or random hugs. They have to catch the next train, hail a cab, squeeze into the first elevator, to ensure they're keeping a leg up. After all, when thousands of people emerge out of the street's subway, the game is on. It's *mano a mano*, you or me, the survival of the fittest in real time. Make it happen fast or die trying. Regardless, Cade always did his best to interrupt the robotic daze.

One particular spring morning, headed north from Tribeca's Chambers Street to Lincoln Center, we'd timed our train ride poorly. Rush hour in Manhattan's subways are from another world. With people crammed in wall-to-wall like sardines, finding a place to hold on was going to be a turf battle. Cade hates standing up in trains. His balance isn't the best, and the way the express trains sway and bounce, he all but demands a seat. On this morning, he was out of luck.

Holding to the center pole, he quietly scanned the seats for any sign of a gap. It didn't need to be much, any sliver of blue fiberglass bench peeking from between two riders, and he'd take his shot. He found it, then darted for a crevice that couldn't have been more than six inches wide. After turning his bottom around, he wedged himself between the hips of two female riders who, until that moment, were minding their own business. The younger brunette to his left, music blasting through her headphones, shot an annoyed glance at Cade. The other, an older lady trying to read a book, recognized Cade's innocent look and obliged.

Cade's a great reader of people's emotions. He's pretty aware that his not-so-sly moves can create annoyances. So after securing his seat, he grinned and tapped the shoulder of the brunette next to him. He offered an exaggerated wave, as if saying, "I'm here now, let's be friends." She noticed his almond-shaped eyes, recognized Cade wasn't your average fare-rider, and allowed herself a kind grin. Sensing a hint of approval, he then made his move, put his arm around her for a side hug, tilted his head, and gave her his biggest smile. She took out her earbuds and started up a cute chitchat.

The older lady realized she was missing out on all the fun and wanted a little of Cade's attention. She shut her book and leaned in for her own side hug, Cade happy to oblige. Cade did what he does best, all smiles and cheering up others. What began as an awkward moment became a rush-hour subway party in real time. It only took Cade a minute, but his courage to break the typical rules of maintaining personal space yet again made him a couple of new friends and brightened their day.

THE SCIENCE OF THE HUG

Physical touch picks me up, but it's not just me. All of us need physical touch. We were made for connection, and when feelings of loneliness, isolation, and depression start to creep in, our bodies long for touch more than ever. A hug can go a long way, and science bears this out. When we hug, our brain releases the neurotransmitter oxytocin, which promotes feelings of contentment and reduces anxiety and stress.[1] In addition, hugging stimulates dopamine and serotonin production in the body and keeps depression at bay.[2] In other words, hugs can be an antidote to our stress and anxiety, and in the long run can stem the threat of depression. Even if it's not Blue Monday—the dreariest day of the year—we could all stand to reduce our stress and anxiety.

At the most primal level, we want to know we are loved and to be reminded of the warmth that surrounds us even in the coldest of seasons. Is it any wonder the majority of birthdays take place in September? The most fertile month in the US is December, a time when mistletoe and touch are at an all-year high![3] The correlation is simple; when it's cold outside, we seek shelter and warmth, and when we feel emotionally cold or isolated (stuck in our own heads), we need the warmth of physical touch.

AT THE MOST PRIMAL LEVEL, WE WANT TO KNOW WE ARE LOVED AND TO BE REMINDED OF THE WARMTH THAT SURROUNDS US EVEN IN THE COLDEST OF SEASONS.

It may sound oversimplified, but maybe we should pay more attention to the way we've been made. God created us for love and comfort, and he wants us to communicate that love and comfort to others. One of the primary ways he allows us to express and receive that love is through physical touch, and maybe it goes without saying, but this expression doesn't always have to be through a hug. *The New York Times* reported in its review of multiple research projects that, "Momentary touches . . . whether an exuberant high five, a warm hand on the shoulder . . . can communicate an even wider range of emotion than gestures or expressions, and sometimes do so more quickly and accurately than words."[4] Not everyone is a hugger, but reaching for the hand of a friend or offering the reassuring squeeze of an arm can sometimes communicate connection better than words.

This was never more apparent than during an unforgettable moment on a treacherous hike Gabe and I navigated during one of our getaway adventures. We were making our way back down from the summit, alongside dozens of other tourists on the trail. With half a mile to go, we bumped into a complete hiker jam—the kind where everyone is stopped and somewhat concerned because a person ahead has been hurt or is incapacitated and cannot move. It was understandable; the path had narrowed in this section to traverse behind a steep waterfall. With danger lurking below, there was hardly room to pass other hikers making their way up. Not knowing what had taken place, it was apparent we might be there for a while.

Gabe could see ahead to where the commotion was, and somehow, we slowly made our way through to see if we could be of some help. As we approached, I saw a group of Muslim women gathered around a young girl with Down syndrome who had completely stopped, frozen in place out of fear and panic. Her mother didn't speak English, no father was in sight, and we could tell the girl was terrified. The rocks were wet, and she was mentally and emotionally stuck, stubbornly committed to not taking another step. Her mother, feeling pressure from other people to get her kid moving, didn't know what to do.

Being the father of a son with Down syndrome, Gabe knelt in front of the girl and looked her in the eyes. With no common language, he grabbed her hands and tenderly assured her it was going to be okay. He then motioned for the girl to climb on his back, quickly scanning up for her mother's approval, unsure if this would break some sort of religious code. The mother nodded her affirmation, and Gabe sat on the ground as the girl climbed on his back. He stood up, held her legs, and she wrapped her arms around his neck, holding on for dear life.

Patiently, step by step, Gabe made his way down the slippery path several hundred feet before reaching a safe plateau. When it was clear we were on better footing, he set the girl down, and fellow hikers passed by. With a smile on her face, all fear having subsided, the little girl reached out to give Gabe a hug. They embraced like they'd known each other for years.

The mother shook Gabe's hand, crying, overwhelmed that a foreign stranger had come to the rescue. In a moment when a little girl was frozen and no one knew what to do, it was the power of physical touch, hand-on-hand reassurance and Gabe's willingness to carry her on his back that provided a breakthrough.

When we experience physical touch from someone else, it communicates more than just their presence. Benedict Carey, a science reporter for *The New York Times* wrote, "In effect, the body interprets a supportive touch as 'I'll share the load.'"[5] Instead of carrying our burdens alone, when we hug each other, when we hold hands, when we offer "supportive touch," we remind each other we don't have to do life alone.

JESUS AND THE POWER OF PHYSICAL TOUCH

Jesus—fully God *and* fully man—knew the power of touch. Throughout the Gospels, he displayed healing power through touch. In Mark 8, he opened the eyes of a blind man through it.[6] In the Gospel of Luke, the writer recorded, "At sunset, the people brought to Jesus all who had various kinds of sickness, and laying his hands on each one, he healed them."[7] Luke also recorded the healing of a woman on the Sabbath this way: "When Jesus saw her, he called her forward and said to her, 'Woman, you are set free from your infirmity.' Then he put his hands on her, and immediately she straightened up and praised God."[8]

Jesus displayed the power of healing touch over and over, but he also used touch as a way of blessing and receiving blessing. In other words, he used it as a mode of human connection. In the Gospel of Luke, Jesus blessed children by placing his hands on them, and in so doing, didn't he connect with the parents who brought the children to him?[9] At a dinner in Bethany, a sinful woman came to Jesus, embraced his legs, and kissed his feet. When the men at the dinner party called off the woman, Jesus said, "You did not give me a kiss, but this woman, from the time I entered, has not stopped kissing my feet."[10] Though the religious men at that dinner party had refused connection with Christ through physical touch, the sinful woman sought it out, and Christ received it. What's more, he released her of her pain, her anxiety, and her sin, saying, "I tell you, her many sins have been forgiven—as her great love has shown."[11] Jesus both used and received the power of touch. Often, the buttoned-up, the more religious among us, pretend to have it all together. We pretend we don't need anything, much less physical touch. If the life of Jesus is any indication, physical touch can be a gateway to healing, blessing, and connection with others and with God. It can bring true freedom from physical anguish and from the anxiety that plagues us in modern life.

———

IF THE LIFE OF JESUS IS ANY INDICATION, PHYSICAL TOUCH CAN BE A GATEWAY TO HEALING, BLESSING, AND CONNECTION WITH OTHERS AND WITH GOD.

———

Maybe you feel like the little girl trapped on the side of the treacherous path, frozen, unsure how to move forward. You've gone as far as you can and now need the tender encouragement of a companion in order to take the next step. Find a loved one—your spouse, a family member, a friend—and ask for a hug. See if it doesn't mute the anxiety, the depression, the pain. And if you know someone who is struggling with depression, anxiety, or panic, offer them a hug (a good, long one). Look them in the eyes, let them know you will walk with them and that they are not alone. See if that kind of physical touch doesn't bring relief.

↗ REFLECTION QUESTIONS ↖

1. WHAT IS YOUR PREFERRED WAY TO USE PHYSICAL TOUCH TO CONNECT WITH A FRIEND? A HUG, A HIGH FIVE, OR A PAT ON THE BACK?

2. HOW DID THE LAST LONG, MEANINGFUL HUG YOU RECEIVED MAKE YOU FEEL?

3. WHO IN YOUR LIFE NEEDS PHYSICAL TOUCH TODAY? FIND THEM. OFFER THEM ENCOURAGEMENT WITH A HIGH FIVE, OR A WARM EMBRACE.

MARRIAGE RETREAT

LOVE THE ONE YOU'RE WITH

CHAPTER 20

MARRIAGE RETREAT

LOVE THE ONE YOU'RE WITH

———

His love motivates her respect; her respect motivates his love.

—EMERSON EGGERICHS

A few years ago, Gabe and I were lying poolside, books in hand. It was our annual getaway, where we could enjoy a bit more quiet than usual with the opportunity to reflect on the year behind and dream about the year ahead. Gabe's book of choice was on marriage, and I took notice. His typical reading list featured books on current issues, spiritual renewal, or historical biography. But this book, *Love and Respect*, had him captivated with how to improve our marriage.

I couldn't help but wonder.

Was something going wrong?

Was he reading about all the ways I should be a better wife?

Would the benefits of his beach read play out today? This week? Next month?

I kept the questions to myself, pushed up my sunglasses, and rested easy knowing my man was going to school.

Marriage can get old. Day after day, we live the same routines, deal with the same bad habits, overreact to the same habitual patterns, and offer the same multiple apologies. It's a wonder anyone stays married their entire life anymore—unless they have found some secret formula.

Our deepest connection in life, if we have the opportunity to experience it, should be with our partner in marriage. Friends are critical, and community is essential, but your spouse plays an out-sized role in contributing to or inhibiting your emotional health. To be clear, we are responsible for our own actions and reactions. No one is to blame for our perspective. But when couples work together, unselfishly love each other, and operate on a united front, there are few things more beautiful. When couples become hurtful and cutting, there are few things more devastating.

OUR DEEPEST CONNECTION IN LIFE, IF WE HAVE
THE OPPORTUNITY TO EXPERIENCE IT, SHOULD
BE WITH OUR PARTNER IN MARRIAGE.

Over the last ten years, Gabe and I hadn't spent much dedicated time working on our marriage. But that's not the way we started. Once, early in our marriage, we attended a church-sponsored marriage retreat, and like everyone else in the world, read *The Five Love Languages*. We were motivated and nervous about getting it right in those initial years. We'd heard the horror stories of marriages getting off track early and didn't want to be another casualty.

But as our kids grew and life became more hectic, time dedicated to receiving outside advice or seeking resources for our marriage went to other things. We assumed if we'd made it this long, we must have something figured out. Occasional date nights and overnight getaways kept us functionally operating on the same page.

Still, we needed to move beyond simply communicating and into a *flourishing* marriage.

A few months after that beach vacation, my friend Joy introduced us to her parents, Emerson and Sarah, at an event. It only took a moment for me to put two and two together: Joy's dad was Emerson Eggerichs, author of *Love and Respect*, the book Gabe had read on our vacation. In our conversation that day, Emerson invited us to come to their home for a visit if we ever wanted marriage counseling or advice. It was an open-door policy, and we tucked that invitation away.

Over the following weeks, I considered Emerson's invitation in light of our marriage. Like most couples, Gabe and I have our fair share of disagreements, and as time passed, we'd experienced new difficult moments in our relationship. Between travel, the demands of parenting adolescents, and multiple work deadlines, we were out of sync. Deeper ruptures surfaced between us that felt new, cutting deep. Yes, we loved each other, but did we *like* each other?

We'd been to therapy, and after a few counseling sessions, we felt better equipped to work through it, but this invitation from Emerson, a marriage guru? We knew we needed to take him up on it. We needed a few days of intensive marriage counsel from a trusted voice who could help us move from maintenance to abundance. So Gabe and I talked it out, scheduled the dates, booked the flights, and made our way to the Eggerichs' Michigan home.

We arrived to a serene lake house setting with a wooded trail that descended to the water's edge, a place I'd find myself praying during the next few days. This gift of time, expertise, and fatherly concern swept us up. What we'd postured as a tune-up (because we were too embarrassed to admit we needed more) turned into a full-fledged exposure, mostly because of Emerson's skillful leadership. We confessed the accusations we'd levied against one another, outed areas of unforgiveness and resentment.

Emerson dove into the grit with us, keeping nothing off-limits. When things were heated, he diffused it all with humor. We laughed as much as we cried, which was so different from our other counseling sessions. The banter, honesty, discipleship, and hospitality Emerson and Sarah displayed over those two days were nothing short of a godsend.

The premise at the heart of what Emerson taught us was quite simple: **Men need respect and women need love.**[1] When that cycle is enacted in a marital relationship, incredible fruit abounds. But when the reverse takes place—a wife disrespecting her husband and a husband failing to respond to the emotional needs of his wife—the crazy cycle unleashes. Fights increase, hurt cuts deep, and spouses emotionally pull away. Once this kind of toxic cycle is in place, it can be hard to correct, and with that cycle comes increased stress, anxiety, and pain.

Gabe and I had been on and off this crazy cycle for too long. Often, I'd express big feelings on a number of topics, and he'd squash them. Emerson challenged Gabe to let me ride this "ocean of emotion," knowing if my fears were heard and understood, they'd dissipate, and I'd move on. But that wasn't the only thing Emerson noted. He addressed our lack of margin, too. We'd bitten off what he called a "ten-pound cheeseburger" in life and were trying not to choke on it. We were investing our lives in good, admirable pursuits, but couldn't find time or energy at the end of a busy day to listen to and understand each other, let alone get to the root of anything, causing distance to grow between us.

Emerson warned against character assassination and disrespect in conflict and told us not to use phrases like "This is who you are," "You always," or "You never" (phrases that are neither true nor helpful). He helped us see how small cracks had become large crevices and we hadn't even realized it. Emerson helped us understand just how our cycle had led us to bitterness, and how bitterness had led us to resentment. Resentment, Emerson said, could suffocate a marriage.

Gabe and I didn't just come to understand the areas of our failings, we began to discover solutions. Confession and the practice of forgiveness can facilitate the healing only God can bring, and late one evening, after an intense conversation, we found ourselves in tears, confessing and forgiving and recommitting ourselves to our marriage. Wiping the slate clean, Gabe's tender heart met mine, a moment I'll never forget.

BUILDING CONNECTION IN MARRIAGE

Marriage—a healthy marriage—has so many known benefits. According to an article in *The Telegraph*, married cancer patients are more likely to survive the disease than their single counterparts.[2] Some research also indicates that being married decreases the risk of heart attack and stroke, encourages safer behavior, lowers stress and anxiety, increases the likelihood of recovery from a major surgery, lowers risk of mental illness, improves sleep, and generally leads to a longer life.[3] With all these benefits, who wouldn't want to cultivate a healthy marriage, even if it takes hard work. Even if it takes admitting your wrongs and extending forgiveness. Even if it takes resetting habits and patterns.

IF OUR RELATIONSHIPS WITH OUR SPOUSES ARE HEALTHY, THEY HELP US CARRY OUR BURDENS, PROCESS CONFUSION, RAISE CHILDREN, AND PARTNER IN OUR WORK.

Our spouses are in our lives each day. If our relationships with our spouses are healthy, they help us carry our burdens, process confusion, raise children, and partner in our work. If our relationships aren't healthy, our marriages bring dis-ease into our lives. The truth is, I hadn't realized how much stress and anxiety my marriage brought into my life, even though it wasn't terrible. That's why Gabe and I have committed to growing in our marriage, to forging healthy practices so our marriage is a safe place to offload stress, not a breeding ground for more stress.

We've made a few changes and are experiencing the benefits. First, every evening, we carve out fifteen minutes to do a quick catch-up on the events of the day—and most important, the emotions attached to them. Whether it's before bed, or on the phone as we run the kids from one commitment to another, we try to get ourselves into each other's shoes and listen for how the other person is processing his or her day. Our goal is to provide perspective, a listening ear, and encouragement, but ultimately, to stay completely caught up on one another's lives so no distance grows from missing out on shared experiences.

Second, we guard our alone time. We look at our calendar every week to ensure we have two hours available for a date with one another. Sometimes this works out as a fun dinner, shopping, or outdoor recreation, but many times it's a breakfast or a lunch while the kids are at school. Of course, this takes away from what can feel like "work time," but we know if we don't stay connected and eye to eye, insecurities creep in, and unintended disconnection is possible.

Finally, we've purposed to let no conflict go unresolved, no matter how short or long the conversation takes. Gabe and I both have strong personalities and passionate opinions. When we have different opinions, the conversation can sometimes go south. But by committing to listen to each other's perspectives, even the most minor disagreements can draw us closer. By offering honest dialogue and hearing with humility, we learn to keep bitterness and resentment at bay.

If your marriage isn't in the healthiest place, be transparent with your spouse. Find a quiet moment when you can open up and share your feelings about your relationship, life, work, and community. Be vulnerable with each other. At first it might feel odd or a bit clunky. Your partner may not respond the way you had hoped or imagined. But when you muster up the courage to speak, to give voice to what you are keeping inside, you begin a journey toward a healthy marriage, a marriage that can bring freedom from the stress and anxiety cycles of the world.

⏶ REFLECTION QUESTIONS ⏷

1. WHEN YOU SHARE YOUR EMOTIONS WITH YOUR SPOUSE, DOES IT HELP YOU OFFLOAD STRESS AND ANXIETY, OR DOES IT INCREASE IT? EXPLAIN YOUR ANSWER.

2. HOW DO YOU DEMONSTRATE LOVE AND RESPECT TO YOUR SPOUSE?

3. IF YOUR MARRIAGE IS A STRESS AND ANXIETY PRODUCER INSTEAD OF A STRESS RELIEVER, WHAT STEP(S) CAN YOU TAKE TO TURN THE TIDE?

APOLOGIZE FIRST

FIRST

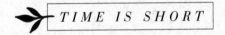
TIME IS SHORT

CHAPTER 21

APOLOGIZE FIRST

TIME IS SHORT

Never forget the nine most important words of any
family—I love you. You are beautiful. Please forgive me.

—H. JACKSON BROWN JR.

T wo months ago, the kids and Gabe and I were on edge. Tensions
tend to surface toward the close of an intense season of exams,
work travel, or book and conference deadlines. It reaches a fever
pitch when there seems to be more responsibility than the number
of hours in the day will allow, and it seems to happen every autumn.

Just before fall exams, I had grand Thursday night plans. It was
our family's only weeknight together between play practice, youth
group, and swim team, and I'd made a home-cooked meal. I tried
to spark conversation at the table, but to no avail. No one had
anything to offer but worn looks and fatigued attitudes. Within

minutes, whatever positive intentions we'd come with disintegrated into finger-pointing and complaining. It happened so fast, Gabe and I were powerless to stop it, so we just sat silently and made eye contact across the table.

Unsure how to salvage the night, we reacted the way we always do when we're unsure what else to do: "Go to your room!" But as our kids mumbled responses and began walking upstairs, hearts more distant with each step, I knew banishing them to their rooms wasn't the right move. Sure, none of us wanted to be together in that moment, and everyone seemed fine with a reprieve. But I knew the best response when connection is broken is not to push away but rather the opposite, to pull in. (After all, wasn't this something Emerson had taught us?)

I yelled up to them, "Stop! Come back to the living room." With eye rolls and complaints about my inconsistent parenting, they returned. Undeterred, I launched into conversation. "None of us feel like being together right now or want to have a conversation about how to address the tension and conflict." The kids didn't say anything, and I imagined them thinking to themselves, *Exactly, so why are we here?*

I continued, "What if we try something else? Let's each find a spot on the couch or a chair and worship together, singing something before God and each other that is good and true. I know singing is the last thing you want to do right now, because it's hard to sing and stay mad. But if we want to reunite our hearts, this might be the best way to work through something instead of faking it and moving on."

Those initial moments following my impassioned monologue were awkward for sure, but no one had a better idea. Pierce, always happy to do the helpful thing, grabbed his guitar and began playing. While the result was disjointed, each person made a whole-hearted attempt, proving their hearts were pliable. Within a few minutes, everyone relaxed and settled into the song. We fixed our focus outside of ourselves and reoriented our hearts.

When the second song came to a close, Gabe and I couldn't get the words out fast enough. We both apologized for our role in the tensions of the evening, taking responsibility for letting the conversation get out of hand. Our kids softened and received our offering. By the end of the third song, they began to open up about their own stress levels, confessing the baggage they'd brought with them into the night, and apologized for their own part in the drama. As our discussion drew to a close, we felt more connected than we had in weeks. Hugs and laughter began to return before bedtime. A night that could have been lost to misunderstanding and frustration was recovered. Our living room moment created true connection and turned into an epic family night!

WHY APOLOGIZE?

Scripture has something to say about going to bed angry: "Do not let the sun go down while you are still angry, and do not give the devil a foothold."[1] I'd heard this statement growing up but never quite understood what a foothold meant. It means a "strong first position from which further progress can be made."[2]

An intruder doesn't need our whole heart, just a crack wide enough to get a foot in the door. When we hold grudges, keeping a record of wrongs against each other time and time again, that crack becomes a wide-open door for the enemy to do what he does best:

"steal and kill and destroy" the ones we love most.[3] Apologizing for the wrongs we've committed paves the way for forgiveness in our relationships.

There's no shortage of research showing the health benefits of extending forgiveness. It lowers blood pressure, stress, and anxiety.[4] It keeps relationships in repair, keeps connectedness strong. But how can you cultivate open, connected, forgiving relationships if you're not willing to be the first to apologize for a misunderstanding? How can you pave the way to wholeness without first apologizing for your part in any brokenness?

APOLOGIZING FOR THE WRONGS WE'VE COMMITTED PAVES THE WAY FOR FORGIVENESS IN OUR RELATIONSHIPS.

I've prioritized confession and apologizing in my own life, believing that *the humility required to apologize restores relationships*. I am teaching my kids to do the same so that they, too, can experience the peace of mind that comes when broken relationships are restored.

TEACHING THE WAY TO OUR KIDS

When I was a young mom, I thought we had forever. The days were long; the entire season seemed infinite. I thought I had plenty of time to teach our kids all the things I wanted them to know.

But now that they are teenagers, I don't want to miss any of it. I want to be a mama who slows down enough to not gloss over conflicts. I want to be proactive in responding to what *wasn't* said. I want to show my kids how to keep from sweeping problems under the rug. After all, I only have so much time left to teach them to apologize for their part in any wrong so that their relationships can be healed, and pain, stress, and anxiety can be relieved. That's why even in tense moments when none of us really wants to talk it out, our family works toward conflict resolution by stopping, confessing, and apologizing. Our commitment to this takes stonewalling off the table and provides a path to healing. Often, that healing connection renews relationships and sucks anger, anxiety, and stress out of the room.

IF YOU KNOW YOU'VE PLAYED A PART IN A BROKEN RELATIONSHIP, WHY NOT LEAD WITH AN APOLOGY?

If you know you've played a part in a broken relationship, why not lead with an apology? Sit down with your spouse or child. Call your loved one or friend. Offer a heartfelt apology and ask for forgiveness. Then, rest easy, knowing you've laid the first stone on the path to restored connections.

↗ REFLECTION QUESTIONS ↖

1. IS THERE A RELATIONSHIP IN YOUR LIFE THAT NEEDS REPAIR? WHAT ARE THE BARRIERS TO MENDING THAT CONNECTION?

2. JOURNAL ABOUT A TIME WHEN YOU EXPERIENCED THE FORGIVENESS OF ANOTHER. HOW DID YOU FEEL AFTERWARD?

3. EVERY APOLOGY DESERVES A FAIR SHOT. IS THERE ANYONE YOU'RE REFUSING TO FORGIVE, EVEN THOUGH THEY'VE APOLOGIZED FOR A WRONG? HOW MUCH ANXIETY AND STRESS DOES THAT BROKEN RELATIONSHIP CAUSE YOU?

CREATE

Having been filled by the input rhythms—having rested and renewed ourselves—and then engaged the first output rhythm of connection, we're fully charged, ready to go into the world and create. When we're full of life, how can we keep from creating?

When I say create, I don't necessarily mean painting, quilting, or composing a song (though it can mean any of those things). Instead, I'm talking about using your specific talents, skills, and callings to live deeper into your God-given purpose, to create something that blesses him and the world around you.

The world's method of creation demands production, striving, and hustle. It is also rooted in self-expression and crowd satisfaction, characteristics diametrically opposed to the holy rhythms of creation. This individualistic form of creative expression often steals our sanity and leads to fits of anxiety, depression, and even addiction.

GOD DIDN'T DESIGN US TO CREATE ON OUR OWN. HE MADE US TO CREATE *WITH* HIM, TO TEND TO HIS CREATION.

God didn't design us to create on our own. He made us to create *with* him, to tend to his creation. When God made men and women (in his own image), he placed them in a garden "to work it and take care of it."[1] He wanted them to work with him in creating something beautiful, something life-giving. That thread of co-creation continues throughout the Old Testament and right into the New. In fact, in his letter to the church at Ephesus, Paul wrote that we are "God's handiwork, created in Christ Jesus to do good works, which God prepared in advance for us to do."[2] See? We were made to be partners with God in his continuing creation. Creation of art? Sure. Creation of kingdom works? Absolutely.

Acts of creation shouldn't be so difficult, and they shouldn't produce constant anxiety. Instead, they should be rooted in the life of God, and as a result, they should bring us peace, life, and rest. They should feel like peace, life, and rest to others, too. So as you read this section, examine the ways you co-create with God and ask yourself these questions:

1. Are my acts of creation marked by the anxiety and stress of the world, or are they seated in the peace and purpose of God? Am I operating from self-expression and crowd satisfaction, or from the deep well of works prepared for me by God himself?

2. Does my painting, crocheting, poetry or (you fill in the blank) _____ bring a sense of peaceful partnership with God?

3. What about the work I'm doing to tend to the hurting (also an act of creation)? Is it marked by striving or by peace?

Are you ready to start co-creating with God? Let's go.

DREAM AGAIN

THE ROAD TO MEANING

CHAPTER 22

DREAM AGAIN

THE ROAD TO MEANING

Life is never made unbearable by circumstances, but only by lack of meaning and purpose.

—VIKTOR FRANKL

I love books by dead people. So much of their prose cuts through the noisy clichés of today. I inhaled *Man's Search for Meaning* five years ago as we traveled through the Irish countryside, through forests and castles and sheep. As I read, I stumbled across Viktor Frankl's words about himself: "The meaning of life is to help others find the meaning of theirs."[1] I read the sentence again, then burst into happy tears. "That's what I want!" I said aloud, grateful for words that leapt off the page, giving language to a yearning in my heart.

Unlike his predecessors, Sigmund Freud (who believed we're made for pleasure) and Alfred Adler (who believed we're made for power), Frankl leaned on his Jewish convictions that men and women were made for meaning. He believed we all desire meaning in three specific categories: work, love, and suffering.

Frankl survived four concentration camps in three years, driven by his convictions, which would form the basis for his life's work, *logotherapy*, the concept that humanity's highest motivating force is the search for meaning. Frankl's premise was that anxiety flows from a life without meaning and purpose. When we lose meaning, we live with a sense of unfulfilled responsibility, rooted in anxiety. With meaning, though, we're free of anxiety. Through freedom, we're given a great responsibility.

As compelling as Frankl's words were, I knew they were an echo of Scripture. I remembered the words of Paul, how he indicated we were called to a free life, a life of meaning. What was the point of our very meaningful, very full lives, though? Paul wrote, "Just make sure that you don't use this freedom as an excuse to do whatever you want to do and destroy your freedom. Rather, use your freedom to serve one another in love; that's how freedom grows."[2]

The freedom we've been given by our Creator has been coupled with the responsibility to serve humanity. When we abdicate this responsibility, our freedom is purposeless. That's why Frankl wrote, "Freedom is in danger of degenerating into mere arbitrariness unless it is lived in terms of responsibleness. That is why I recommend that the Statue of Liberty on the East Coast be supplemented by a Statue of Responsibility on the West Coast."[3] In the landscape of today, many people—women in particular—don't realize the purpose and value they bring to the world. Whether it's because of family norms, traditional understandings of gender roles, or societal pressure, women have grown used to conforming to a shadow of who they were designed to be. And we wonder why so many women struggle with anxiety, stress, and depression.

THE OBSTACLES TO DREAMING AND MEANING

As Frankl points out, many of us never find the deeper meaning of our lives and push into our dreams because we live in a culture of affluence and boredom. By virtue of being American citizens, we are wealthy compared to the rest of the world. A Pew Research Center study shows that "almost nine-in-ten Americans (have) a standard of living that (is) above the global middle-income standard."[4] Many of us drive cars, eat regular meals, and have an assortment of clothing. In those terms, we are affluent. And our wealth affords us the luxury of entertainment. Often, when we aren't entertained, we're bored. Our solution to boredom? More entertainment, please.

There are indeed exceptions. Some of us work hard to survive, and who has time to be bored as a single mother working two jobs? But in general, if we have too much time on our hands, too little responsibility, and not enough entertainment, we're headed into a crisis of identity and anxiety.

Perhaps most mentally destabilizing, and therefore most concerning, is our boredom. A recent *Time* article reported, "American youth, especially teens, are not in good emotional shape. They feel mostly 'bored and checked out' at school, according to adolescence scholar Larry Steinberg. Academically, they are underachieving when compared to youth in other developed nations, and their mental health is declining. During the school year, their stress has edged beyond that of adults." [5]

BREAKING THROUGH BOREDOM
AND THE DESIRE TO ESCAPE

But this isn't just true of teenagers. It's true of many adults, too. We're stuck in a culture of boredom, one which keeps us chasing entertainment, and we have so many entertaining options—video games, streaming services, hand-held devices. No matter our age, dreams get squashed when our lives are consumed with entertainment and technology. As Neil Postman predicted in his prophetic work from 1985, *Amusing Ourselves to Death*, "People will come to adore the technologies that undo their capacities to think."[6] I might put it another way: People *have* come to adore the technologies that undo their capacities to *dream*.

How do you escape the dream-killing trap of boredom? What are some strategies to overcome the draw to easy entertainment? Consider taking a break from your go-to form of escape. When you'd rather start a Netflix binge or turn to social media, grab a pen and a piece of paper instead. (See how the rhythms of create dovetail with the rhythms of rest?) Sit in the silence and dream. Imagine what you want your life to look like in five or ten years— your vocation, your service opportunities. Picture the future you want for yourself, your marriage, your kids. Ask yourself: *Who am I meant to be? What am I meant to do?*

WHO AM I MEANT TO BE? WHAT AM I MEANT TO DO?

When I did this exercise and took time to dream, it brought new dreams to light. New possibilities became realities as I began to walk into those dreams, one small step at a time. I began churning out words, writing to inspire women in their relationships with God. I began traveling and speaking on panic and anxiety, helping women overcome their fears. With each step in this new direction, you know what I found? More meaning and purpose.

But what if you make the time, sit with a pad and paper, and can't come up with any dreams? Take yourself back to age ten and reflect for a moment.

What did you love to do most when you were eight, nine, ten?

What talents were obvious to those around you?

Why did you stop?

The answers to these questions can offer clues and insight into your hardwiring, into who you are meant to be and what you are meant to do. Believe it or not, what brought you to life as a pre-teen is connected to what will awaken you now. It may play out in a different form, but there is gold in mining the dreams of your youth. Throughout elementary school, I was obsessed with reading books. One summer, I read every single Encyclopedia Brown book in the collection. I loved the feeling of accomplishment when I solved the mystery or closed the back cover. I thought then that people who write books must love their jobs, and today, I write books. See how the passions of my youth gave insight to my dreams, my purpose?

But boredom and escape aren't the only obstacles we need to push through in order to find meaning and pursue our dreams.

CREATING SPACE FOR DREAMING

As I travel the country and speak with women of all ages, as I engage with them online, women who've been relegated to the sidelines as they've tended to children, or served in administrative positions, or were minimized in their influence are asking questions like, *How do I imagine a life of purpose when there seems to be so little time?*

It's a question I've asked before, too, and each time I hear it, it strikes a deep chord. As a young mom, it was difficult for me to navigate my roles as wife, mother, and friend. Motherhood demands so much, and in those early years, it can be hard to find time to accomplish much beyond changing diapers, doing laundry, and organizing playdates. I used to think I ought not consider placing my energy anywhere beyond the four walls of home. Of course, this is generally reasonable advice to a mother of three, including one with special needs. But what I didn't realize then was that my contribution doesn't have to be an either/or thing. It can be both/and.

How?

Gabe and I look for active ways to support each other in the callings God's put on our lives. We share the responsibilities of managing a household: laundry, cooking and cleaning, running errands, paying bills, doing dishes, helping with homework. If he needs to go to the grocery store, he goes. If I need to call the plumber, I do. We don't have arbitrary rules about what we do and don't contribute to help our family run. Whatever is needed in the moment, either of us will jump in to supply.

This also goes for nurturing our kids' hearts. In our philosophy of marriage and parenting, Gabe and I share the same priorities. My primary focus as a wife and mother is the well-being of my husband and children. Gabe's primary focus as a husband and father is on me and the children. Work, other friendships, hobbies, and travel come after. That's the deal—for both of us—and because we don't put constraints around how we contribute to the family, we don't put constraints around our dreams, either. If one of us has a dream that's important, that's worth chasing, the other helps make that happen. Gabe was my biggest supporter as I pushed into writing and speaking. As I shared earlier, he's pulled more weight in our home as I've pushed into my calling.

I recognize every relational circumstance looks different. Whether you are single, parenting alone, or in a marriage where your spouse isn't interested in mutual support, you have unique obstacles to living out your dreams. But with a little imagination, a little nurturing of the dream, a little collaboration with your spouse, children, or friends, you just might find a path through those obstacles.

A DREAM OF MEANING

As Frankl noted, much of our anxiety and stress is created by the purposelessness of our lives. In that purposelessness, we drift from entertainment to entertainment, never finding the peace and fulfillment we need. We lose time and energy because busyness distracts us from the most important things. But if there's one thing that's certain, it's that we were made for more. We were designed to dream, and to take responsibility for those dreams. We were made for meaning.

———

WE WERE DESIGNED TO DREAM, AND TO TAKE
RESPONSIBILITY FOR THOSE DREAMS.

———

The act of creating doesn't come from nowhere. It begins with a dream, and when we tap into our dreams, when we walk forward in them, God gives us renewed meaning and purpose. Knowing God's meaning and purpose for our lives frees us from stress and anxiety, but it can also bring freedom to the world.

↗ REFLECTION QUESTIONS ↖

1. IF WE WERE RIDING AN ELEVATOR TOGETHER, AND I GAVE YOU TWO MINUTES TO DESCRIBE YOUR DREAMS TO ME, WHAT WOULD YOU SAY?

2. WHAT DREAMS OR PASSIONS DID YOU HAVE AS A CHILD?

3. IF YOU AREN'T PURSUING YOUR DREAMS OR PASSIONS, WHY NOT?

RECOVER YOUR PASSION

PULLING WEEDS

CHAPTER 23

CHAPTER 23

RECOVER YOUR PASSION

PULLING WEEDS

The two most important days in your life are the day you are born and the day you find out why.

—MARK TWAIN

Looking across the front yard of our new country home, it became clear—we'd underestimated what managing a sprawling piece of Tennessee property might require. We loved the idea of rolling hills and a view, but when spring swept in with near-daily rain, moving a little further out came with a list of outside chores that never seemed to end.

On my first Saturday home after two weekends of travel, I woke early. I had forty-eight hours to reconnect with Gabe and our kids, and to help out with what felt most urgent around the house, and then I had to head back out to speak again. I brewed a pot of coffee and, with steaming mug in hand, ventured to the rockers on the front porch. Once seated, I couldn't avoid noticing the weeds taking over the front and sides of our house. Many were taller than I, blowing in the wind. The tangled green thicket of undesirables, so many varieties, was enough to hide the flower beds altogether. It looked as if our house had been abandoned overnight.

I couldn't distinguish the flowering perennials from the flowering weeds, though many of the plants we loved and wanted to keep were hidden below the chaos. I vaguely remembered some sort of strategic design by the original owner, but her intentions had become invisible, hidden, of no benefit to anyone now. I decided then and there that I was going to clear out those weeds over my two days at home.

The magnitude of the weeding project both inspired and terrified me. Could I clear the weeds in two days while I was home? What was left starving for sunlight underneath? I didn't know, but I felt up to the challenge for reasons I couldn't yet understand.

By nine o'clock, the air was fully saturated, so humid you could almost swim in it. I didn't give up, though. I needed something physical after all the travel, all the sitting on planes, in cars, in conferences. I wanted to get my hands dirty and see tangible results. After two hours, I was making progress but still had a long way to go. I looked down at my hands. My old gloves were ripped and soaked from wet leaves and dirt left behind by the storm the night before, and there were more nettles to pull, more thorny things I couldn't name. Looking for reprieve, I scurried to Tractor Supply.

Thirty minutes later, I donned a new pair of gloves and dove back in. I pulled and pulled, my lower back sore and knees aching from the constant crouching and shuffling. Still, I kept going, staying focused on the task. I didn't look up, didn't check the messages on my phone or run in for a break and another cup of coffee. I just kept pulling the weeds, sometimes one by one, sometimes grabbing a mass of stems and pulling them up by the roots. The root was always the goal, however deep it might be. Removing the root was the only way to prevent the weed's return.

The morning hours were running out, and the heat was beginning to dry and harden the ground, so I pushed myself to the point of dizziness several times. Gabe saw my stubborn persistence and jumped in to help, afraid I'd pass out all alone. (This is what it means to be together for better or for worse!)

As I neared the end of all that pulling, something happened. I started to see the shape of the previous owner's strategy. The original curves of the flowerbeds emerged, boxwoods began to stand tall in pretty rows, and sporadic patches of mulch found the light of day for the first time in weeks.

Little by little, order returned, and it was beautiful. Never had outdoor work felt so fulfilling. I was six hours in, and there was no stopping now. I pushed through another two hours. Then three. I felt passionate about what was being uncovered, about beauty being restored, inspired by what I'd create again in these flower beds once we made room for new life to emerge.

I barely noticed the setting sun until Gabe pointed it out. We had evening plans; he'd come out to tell me it was time to get ready. I hated to leave, but I knew I needed a break. My body couldn't take any more dizzy spells, any more crouching and pulling, and after our dinner that night, I sank onto my bed, exhausted and grateful. I couldn't wait to get back to it the next morning.

I woke on Sunday at six. I could hardly move, but I'd set my sights on finishing. I popped some ibuprofen to fend off the pain, put on my new turquoise gloves, applied sunscreen to my cheeks and neck, threw on my black baseball hat, and headed out the door.

In the early morning quiet, as I worked and listened to the chorus of my early bird friends, I thought of my dad and how he always puttered around the yard with projects. He always preferred to be outside tending the garden, sitting in the grass pulling weeds, donning his signature triangle hat made out of newspaper to offer extra shade. From time to time he'd pull something from the dirt and taste it. He'd sample anything that grew on anything, including every part of an apple except the stem. I suppose I got my love for gardening, for nature, for anything outdoors, from him.

As I kept working that garden, I remembered telling my friend a couple of weeks prior that I was in the middle of a foundation-shifting season, and the metaphor of clearing the dirt foundation bordering our home was not lost on me. Never had I been so excited to tackle a project, much less with such a sense of urgency, but here I was, spending the only two days I had at home that week in the blazing sun as if my life depended on it.

My excitement about working in the yard that weekend was a tangible expression of how I used to feel about my work. In the beginning, I was passionate to write and teach with energy to spare, coming up with new ideas and concepts each day and even into the night. God would press thoughts onto my heart, and I'd jot them down as quickly as they came. But over the years, that passion began to wane. I wanted that endless energy back, where I'd pour over volumes of research and study for long hours, my nose buried in books. I wanted to recover the same kind of passion and energy for writing and teaching as I found that weekend clearing weeds.

I wanted to recover the passion that surrounded my vocation.

PULLING PASSION-CHOKING WEEDS

Each of us is made for something specific, given a particular passion by God so we can partner with him in creating and constructing the Kingdom. It's a belief backed by Scripture, which indicates that each of us has a different role, a different passion.[1] When we discover that passion, when we live into it, we become more alive. Nothing has been more emboldening, more fulfilling, more true for me than living out my passion: helping people live out their calling from a place of freedom.

> EACH OF US IS MADE FOR SOMETHING SPECIFIC, GIVEN A PARTICULAR PASSION BY GOD SO WE CAN PARTNER WITH HIM IN CREATING AND CONSTRUCTING THE KINGDOM.

Yet in recent years, I had allowed other things to crowd out my one specific thing, the greatest thing. I said yes to speaking at conferences, even if the topic wasn't a direct fit. I'd spread myself too thin with activities at home as well, and felt like I was always moving from one thing to the next. Then there was social media. How many times had I found myself in the middle of a hot mess on Twitter or a dumpster fire discussion on a Facebook thread? Many distractions overtook the simplicity of the call. Over time I began to lose sight of my early passion and zeal, and I found myself on the edge of burnout.

The day I told my mother-in-law I was losing my passion—not a phrase I could ever imagine saying—I knew I needed to do something about it. So just as I'd pulled weeds in the garden, I pulled the distractions away, one by one, for fear they'd forever suffocate my passion. The social media distractions, additional obligations, pressures, and stressors. All those things had crept in without me realizing it, and they'd overtaken the life I'd intended to grow in the first place. They caused low-grade anxiety, too, though I hadn't realized it until I got rid of them. As I cleared space, as I gained margin, my passion was reignited. I began to dive into challenging books. I jotted down new ideas during afternoon walks. I found myself writing and teaching with renewed excitement when I made room again for what I was created to do, and began to thrive once more.

CLEAR THE WEEDS CHOKING YOUR PASSION

What's choking your passion, your work, the place where your creative energy was meant to go? What things do you need to pull from your life so you have the energy to partner with God in his creative purpose for you? Identify those things and get rid of them: activities that don't bring life, distracting obligations, or social media. Pull the weeds. Get them at the root so they don't grow back. Then, with renewed passion, use your passion to create something beautiful with God.

WHAT'S CHOKING YOUR PASSION, YOUR WORK, THE PLACE
WHERE YOUR CREATIVE ENERGY WAS MEANT TO GO?

↗ REFLECTION QUESTIONS ↖

1. WHAT ARE YOU MOST PASSIONATE ABOUT? IS IT SOME MINISTRY ENDEAVOR? A KIND OF ART? AN ASPECT OF YOUR CAREER? DO YOU KNOW? SPEND SOME TIME EXPLORING YOUR PASSION, AND JOURNAL YOUR RESPONSES.

2. WHAT DISTRACTIONS ARE CHOKING YOUR PASSIONS, YOUR ENERGY TO CREATE?

3. HOW WILL YOU EMPLOY YOUR PASSION TO CREATE SOMETHING BEAUTIFUL WITH GOD?

WORK WITH YOUR HANDS

A PATTERN AND A PLAN

CHAPTER 24

WORK WITH YOUR HANDS

A PATTERN AND A PLAN

———

Live a quiet life and work with your hands.

—DANA TANAMACHI

I grew up watching my mama sew. She'd bought a repossessed Touch & Sew in 1965 from the Singer store downtown. To get the money for the down payment, she'd sold her old machine to a neighbor and worked as a bank teller to pay off the rest. It was stored in a wooden cabinet, with a foot pedal and special discs to make fancy zig-zags. The whir of this magical machine was the melodic backdrop of my upbringing. The sewing machine was always running because, between the six of us, there was always a pile of shirts or pants that needed mending, or a pattern and fabric waiting to bring a new outfit to life.

As the oldest daughter in our family, I was the perfect candidate to model my mama's craftsmanship and flair. She made dress after dress for me in bold, colorful patterns, and because she's nostalgic like that, she even sewed a blanket with large letters spelling out R-E-B-E-K-A-H appliqued on it, each letter reflecting a different fabric from a dress she'd made me. This blanket remains one of my most treasured gifts.

I was ten when I finally received a green light to make my first garment on Mama's sewing machine. I spent a great deal of time considering what I would make for my first independent project. I landed on a sleeveless blouse with pink and blue stripes (these were my colors because I was a "Summer") with a scalloped hemline that would land just below my waist. The back closure was held fast with pink, heart-shaped buttons. I thought a sleeveless pattern would be easiest. Turns out it wasn't. I became quite familiar with terms like *piping* and *interfacing* before the project was complete. At long last, my sewing skills took center stage when I wore this beauty with some culottes to the first day of summer sleep-away camp.

Over the next twenty years, I continued to take on sewing projects. Among the items I made were four high school homecoming dresses, a mauve and forest green bedspread for my college dorm room, and a prom dress for one of my first dates with Gabe. I liked the freedom to create any look I wanted at little cost, and once I'd figured out the building blocks of sewing, the creative process of working with my hands felt almost therapeutic. What seemed like good, creative fun all those years was actually the critical thinking of craftsmanship. Once I understood how each step built upon the last, I would become laser-focused, humming a tune or biting my lip.

Sewing wasn't the only way my mama taught us to work with our hands. Every Christmas we made handmade felt ornaments for our friends and extended family. We'd select a new pattern annually, cut it out using different colors of felt, layer and assemble it all with a hot glue gun, and then attach a loop for hanging. One year, the chosen ornament was a tiny stocking with a note tucked inside.

For our birthdays, we teamed up with Mom to create a cake for the birthday boy or girl. We chose a recipe from a cake pattern book, and with round or rectangle pans, a pattern to trace, and a butter knife, we decorated cakes in every shape, from a race car to an angel to a butterfly.

The way our family operated taught me something important: you can make just about anything with patience, a pattern, and a little attention to detail.

When Gabe and I married, I took to the art of making window treatments like it was my job. It was my way of creating beauty and saving some cash. This was the era when cornice boards were a hit, so I took to buying the foam, cutting the shape, and getting reacquainted with a hot glue gun. This decorating frenzy spiraled into sewing draped end table covers, pillow shams and comforters for each bed, and, yes, I even took on the daunting task of reupholstering vintage armchairs and an old sofa with a trusty staple gun. With a small budget and lots of time (we didn't have kids yet), I wanted to create a cozy home with personal flair.

Once I'd covered every surface possible with fabric, next was paint. One weekend when Gabe was traveling, I got the brilliant idea to paint our bedroom bright red, *by myself*, to surprise him when he returned home. It wasn't a wise color choice for a solo amateur, but I was determined. Hours later, the wall was covered with streaks and my arm was about ready to fall off. That's how I learned that red wall paint is unforgiving. When Gabe arrived home, he helped me put on another coat. It never really looked streak-free, but it was ours.

THE JOY OF WORKING WITH YOUR HANDS

I look back on those years of working with my hands and see how it offered a sense of accomplishment and grew my confidence. It helped me believe I could do anything, and there was a satisfaction in being a lifelong learner, in being up for any challenge, even if it required risk. Working with my hands taught me spatial awareness and how to layer a color palette in a room, from walls to linens to art. Later in our marriage, it taught me how to make the most of every square inch of our 1,100-square-foot New York City apartment. What's more, whenever anxiety arose, I could always turn to some creative effort with my hands, and I'd find relief.

The stress-and anxiety-relieving aspects of working with our hands have been documented. According to *Psychology Today*, "Research has shown that hand activity from knitting to woodworking to growing vegetables or chopping them are useful for decreasing stress, relieving anxiety, and modifying depression . . . Functioning hands also foster a flow in the mind that leads to spontaneous joyful, creative thought. Peak moments occur as one putters, ponders and daydreams."[1] What's more, one online publication noted that "[D]octors in the 19th century would prescribe knitting to anxiety-ridden women. Without knowing the exact neuroscience behind it, they did know that knitting somehow relaxed these patients."[2] In a very real sense, working with our hands relieves the mind.

IN A VERY REAL SENSE, WORKING WITH
OUR HANDS RELIEVES THE MIND.

Maybe it's just me, but it seems that in this ultra-busy, highly-automated, computer-oriented world, we work with our hands less and less. We busy ourselves cranking out drafts and reports, and poring over spreadsheets. Instead of making clothes, we buy them. Instead of reupholstering our own chairs, we pay someone else to do it. Is it any wonder, then, that we have so much stress and anxiety? I suspect if those 19th-century doctors visited today's culture, they'd give us a simple prescription for our anxiety and panic: go make something.

MAKE A PLAN TO MAKE

Creating something with your hands (like a sweater, or loaf of bread, or piece of art) won't happen without planning and preparation. You'll need to identify what it is that you want to create (whatever it is, the making of it should be joy-filled and non-anxious). Consider exploring an old hobby, like sewing, or trying something new, like calligraphy or watercolor painting. Look for new ideas on Pinterest or at your local craft or fabric store, and pick the brains of your creative friends.

Once you identify what you want to create, you might need to find a pattern or download a set of instructions or find a DIY video on YouTube. Then, set aside the time to create. Since we only have twenty-four hours every day, this usually means finding a day I can unplug online, which frees up extra time to be fully present and immerse myself in tackling something new without distraction.

Creating something from scratch can sometimes feel daunting, but when we're engaged in the act itself, we'll find release from the stress, depression, and anxiety of the world outside. I know this firsthand. My daughter does, too. Kennedy was in the middle of a tough season, and I asked her if it would help to create something with her hands. She said yes, so we went to a craft store and bought a cheap, twin memory foam mattress on clearance and a dozen bottles of puffy paint. When we got home, she got after it, cutting the mattress into different shapes and painting those shapes. She created squishies (foam objects meant to be squeezed for stress relief) all weekend, maybe enough to give one to every sixth grader in town, and by the end of the weekend, her stress and anxiety had dissipated.

USING OUR HANDS, EMPLOYING OUR GOD-GIVEN CREATIVITY TO MAKE SOMETHING NEW, IS GOOD MEDICINE FOR THE SOUL.

Using our hands, employing our God-given creativity to make something new, is good medicine for the soul. It helps us to focus on something other than ourselves and use our strategic problem-solving skills to create something that brings beauty and builds our confidence as creators. It fills us with a sense of accomplishment and often allows us to offer the world a gift. Today, make a plan to make something. Gather the materials, carve out the time, and enjoy it.

↗ REFLECTION QUESTIONS ↖

1. WHEN IS THE LAST TIME YOU MADE SOMETHING WITH YOUR HANDS?

2. WHEN YOU WERE FINISHED, HOW DID YOU FEEL?

3. WHAT'S ONE THING YOU'VE ALWAYS WANTED TO CREATE
   WITH YOUR HANDS? WHAT STEPS WILL YOU TAKE IN THE NEXT
   MONTH TO START CREATING?

LEARN
SOMETHING
NEW

TAKE A CLASS

CHAPTER 25

LEARN SOMETHING NEW

TAKE A CLASS

Anyone who stops learning is old, whether at twenty or eighty.

—HENRY FORD

Two months after arriving in New York City, we sent our youngest off to kindergarten. Just like that, our proverbial decade of weekdays at the library for story time, food court lunches, and children's museum playdates had drawn to a close.

WHEN WE ARE UNCERTAIN ABOUT OUR PLACE
IN THE WORLD, FEAR CAN SETTLE IN.

I wasn't sad about this shift, though I felt the void. Looking back,

I wonder if the anxiety I experienced that first year in Manhattan could be traced back to my not knowing what to do now that I had time. When we are uncertain about our place in the world, fear can settle in, and that's what happened to me. When faced with a clean slate, all I had were questions:

Do I even deserve to spend time on myself?

What would I focus on in this new season?

How should I spend my newfound time?

Where do I start?

It had been so long since I had time to consider what I enjoyed, what I wanted to do most. So I took inventory. Over the last decade, while not dealing with diapers, I loved reading up on the latest in fashion and interior design. Not because I had a professional interest in design, mind you. Instead, it provided an escape into adult land. Even so, my fascination with all things design was a clue into an area of untapped potential.

Manhattan has some of the leading design schools in the country, so I looked up Parson's School of Design to see what type of extended learning classes they offered. Taking a class was something I'd avoided since my college days, but at this stage of my life, it was what I needed. Stepping back into formal education had a different appeal now, and it turned out Parson's had a fall class starting in just two weeks, The Fundamentals of Fashion Design. Two years prior to our move to New York City, I'd tried a brief stint designing dresses for a children's line in Atlanta. Though I enjoyed it, the job taught me that I didn't know what I didn't know. With many of our friends working in some area of the fashion industry, I was curious to learn the fundamentals of design from the experts. So I took a deep breath and registered.

Every Friday evening, Gabe would care for the kids, and I'd jump on a train from Lexington and 59th to ride downtown to Union Square. Although I was in my mid-thirties, I couldn't wait to join the other creatives, designers, and artistic types, who were a lot like me but about half my age. I was grateful a friend a decade younger decided to take the same course that fall semester. She kept us laughing and helped me bridge the age gap.

The Fundamentals of Fashion Design entailed fashion design history, drawing fashion flats, sketching live models, and doing a little costume design. I learned I was awful at sketching and had had no idea how important this skill was for bringing a design into being. I felt pushed and completely out of my comfort zone. I'd imagine something in my mind but could not bring it to life on the page. Every week we'd sketch models walking the runway, in quick and repetitive turnarounds. The goal was speed and efficiency—and proficiency. If we could imagine the movements of fabric over the body, we could be better designers. My results? Let's just say I was mortified by them.

Day after day we sat at tables placed in a U-shape with the runway set up in the center. As our professor circled the desks to preview our work, I always tried to cover mine with my left arm (one of the benefits of being left-handed) to avoid public embarrassment. After all, our instructor was happy to offer loud feedback (read: criticism) in front of the entire group. If one student could learn from her mistakes, why shouldn't everyone? I kept my head down and kept quiet.

Redemption came toward the end of the semester, though. We finally moved past the sketch and conceptualizing phase to pattern-making and sewing, areas where my childhood sewing lessons enabled me to shine. Along with the other students, my final grade would be based on an outfit I designed, sewed, and modeled for the class. I found my groove and made a soft, gray woolen dress with fitted bodice and pleated skirt. When I modeled it for the class of mostly twenty-year-olds, they gave me affirming applause—impressed that this old girl just might have a little *Vogue* in her after all.

Learning something new had a profound impact on my confidence. If I hadn't taken that class, I wouldn't have had the courage to try other new things. Later that same year, I wrote my first article, which led to another, then another, and ultimately a first book. At a quick glance, there may not seem to be a correlation between Parsons School of Design and becoming a published author, but there was a deep connection. My push to learn something new helped me believe I could still create, even if it was in an unfamiliar field. It helped me believe I could tell stories, encourage others, and create something substantial.

Looking back now, even though I didn't become a fashion designer, I'm glad I explored designing with open hands. If I hadn't followed my curiosity, who knows whether I would have believed in myself enough to write those articles? Who knows whether I'd be writing this book now?

THE ARTIST DATE

There are so many ways to learn something new. Taking a class is a more formal way, but one of my favorite ways of learning something new is something author Julia Cameron calls "The Artist Date." She writes,

> The Artist Date is a once-weekly, festive, solo expedition to explore something that interests you. The Artist Date need not be overtly "artistic"—think mischief more than mastery. Artist Dates fire up the imagination. They spark whimsy. They encourage play. Since art is about the play of ideas, they feed our creative work by replenishing our inner well of images and inspiration.[1]

Our brains benefit when we put ourselves in new environments. The scientific term for it is *neuroplasticity*—the understanding that "intelligence is not fixed, it turns out, nor planted firmly in our brains from birth. Rather, it's forming and developing throughout our lives."[2] When we give ourselves new experiences, we begin to expand our thinking and creativity. New electrochemical pathways are formed, like highways that connect past experiences and knowledge to new ones. But the opposite is true as well. When we stop pushing ourselves to learn, our brain suffers. "When people stop practicing new things, the brain will eventually eliminate, or 'prune,' the connecting cells that formed the pathways."[3] The more connections we can create, the better, because we are always either connecting or disconnecting.

WHEN WE GIVE OURSELVES NEW EXPERIENCES,
WE BEGIN TO EXPAND OUR THINKING AND CREATIVITY.

This brings us back to learning a new creative outlet. When we are depressed, anxious, or lonely, it can be a reflection of an unhealthy turn inward. We become sad about who we are or how life is falling short of our expectations. Feeling helpless in the face of these emotions, we self-soothe with a bag of popcorn, a warm furry blanket, and the latest episode of our favorite series on Hulu. We want to do anything but learn something new! But this is an essential practice if we are going to live lives of peace and purpose.

During that first year in Manhattan, God knew that making it through those anxious days and panic-stricken moments required, in part, an expanding vision of what I was capable of doing. But that expanded vision would never have come without the courage that came with learning something new.

If you are in a dreary season and barely putting one foot in front of the other, you're not alone. I know how it feels. The last thing you want to hear is that you need to take on one more thing. But trust me, if you take the courageous step to learn something new, you'll find new pathways to freedom, pathways that lead you to become who you were meant to be.

↗ REFLECTION QUESTIONS ↖

1. ARE YOU THE KIND OF PERSON WHO TRIES NEW THINGS, OR DO YOU STICK WITH WHAT YOU KNOW? WHEN'S THE LAST TIME YOU ENROLLED IN A CLASS, PICKED UP A NEW HOBBY, OR TRIED SOME NEW ACTIVITY? WHAT DID YOU LEARN?

2. HOW DID IT MAKE YOU FEEL?

3. PLAN AN ARTIST DATE IN THE NEXT MONTH. WHAT WILL IT
   BE? JOURNAL YOUR IDEA.

MAKE A MEMORY

IMAGINATIVE PLAY

CHAPTER 26

MAKE A MEMORY

IMAGINATIVE PLAY

Memories aren't made from to-do lists.

—AEDRIEL MOXLEY

Each year during the holidays, our family pulls out the home movies, loads a bowl with truffle-salt popcorn, and settles in for our absolute favorite trilogy of the year: *Honey, I Shrunk the Kids*; *Honey, I Blew Up the Kids*; and *Star Wars*. No, I'm not talking about the feature films that made over a billion dollars at the box office. I'm talking about the short films inspired by them, starring the Lyons family, circa 2006–2007.

As new parents in our twenties with almost no energy to spare, Gabe and I received some valuable advice from Mark and Jan Foreman, our mentors and friends, who had managed to raise their kids to become creative adults. Mark and Jan championed one big idea:

when our children come to us with a crazy idea of an experience they'd like to create, our answer should always be yes.

At age four Pierce wanted to make films, and what better place to start than our basement? The first short film would be *Honey I Blew Up the Kids*. Cade was the baby, Kennedy was the babysitter, Pierce was the professor, and Gabe and I were, well, the parents. The growing machine was our vacuum with its detachable suction tube and the Hot Wheels cars and racetrack made up the city once Cade was blown up. In five short minutes, after terrorizing the faux city, Cade was shrunk back down to a normal size and reunited with his mom and dad in our minivan in the garage, all while the cameras kept rolling.

Then came the Luke Skywalker lightsaber phase. Wearing a sash, my brown western boots, and a fuzzy eye mask strapped around his head for a beard, five-year-old Pierce played Luke. I was Princess Leia with two braided side buns and a white bathrobe. The costume designer must have called in sick. Cade was the villain in a voice-activated Darth Vader helmet and Gabe's black coat. My favorite scene is the finale, where Luke brags to Leia how he was "pushin' 'im and shovin' 'im" (Darth) until victory was won, all while drinking a can of Coke.

Once Pierce got over his aspirations of being a filmmaker, he decided he'd become a professional baseball player when he grew up. So we concocted the Braves' baseball stadium on our backyard patio. With a load of sidewalk chalk and empty Rubbermaid storage containers, we crafted the dugout, the outfield, the bleachers, even the Coke bottle, which was displayed high on a ledge. Donning a Braves' jersey and baseball hat, Pierce stepped up to the T-ball set while adoring fans cheered loudly. He even broke the home run record that year! This game lasted off and on for a few weeks, constantly redrawn on the patio or brought into our living room if there was a rain delay.

There was no limit to what Gabe would say yes to. When Pierce asked to build a roller coaster in our back yard a couple of years later, Gabe responded, "Sure, we'll get to that when you're twelve." Gabe thought by twelve Pierce would be old enough to understand this was an unreasonable request. *He did not.* So Gabe had to break the news that the roller coaster would take on more of a trampoline-like round shape instead.

Saying yes became the way we engaged with our children. It challenged us to be creative, even when they asked for improbable experiences like building roller coasters or making feature films. But it also offered me something just as valuable—especially on rough days when I didn't feel like getting out of bed. I was motivated to push apathy to the side as Pierce or Kennedy or Cade asked me to wear silly costumes or join in their wild creativity. Self-absorption faded when I put myself in their shoes in an attempt to offer a memorable experience.

———

WHEN WE BREAK OUT OF THE CYCLE OF DRUDGERY AND FOCUS ON CREATING MEMORIES WITH THOSE AROUND US, WE START TO FIND THE WONDER IN LIFE.

———

Imagination precedes creativity.[1] In other words, if we can't imagine well, we limit our potential for new creative ideas and live constrained by our old rhythms. When we break out of the cycle of drudgery and focus on creating memories with those around us, we start to find the wonder in life.

MEMORIES AREN'T MADE FROM TO-DO LISTS

Unless you *actually* enjoy memories of grocery store runs, school carpool line pick-ups, and cleaning out the garage, my dear friend Aedriel Moxley is right: memories aren't made from the to-do list. A to-do list requires little creativity, though checking the boxes helps us feel like we've accomplished something significant.

In an article in *Fast Company*, Reva Seth writes, "Many of the actions on our to-do lists—those that govern our daily lives—don't actually correspond to our main values. And that only exacerbates the feeling of being overwhelmed."[2] I know this from experience. There are days when I put all of my best energy into what I call "robotic activities"—tasks that require no imagination or special talent but are required to keep a house and family running. If this becomes the only place my energy goes day after day, it leaves me lifeless. Even if I check off everything on the list, I still feel depleted and exhausted when my head hits the pillow.

When we sacrifice the values we cherish most for the immediacy of checking things off our lists, we do ourselves harm. Our hearts need space to feel, create, embrace, and love—none of which can be placed on a to-do list. These priorities only come when we make time for exploration, fun, and unexpected life to happen.

While doing research for this book, I came across an account detailing Leonardo Da Vinci's life as observed through his journals. His to-do list was comprised of items like "Draw Milan" (yes, the entire city!) and "ask Maestro Antonio how mortars are positioned on bastions by day or night," an architectural inquiry he was considering.[3] Da Vinci's daily tasks were fueled by passionate pursuits and meaningful conversations that would sharpen his mind and expand his imagination. If I had my guess, I would say his imaginative thinking led to more than a few memories during his lifetime.

MEMORIES INSPIRE OTHERS

When we make memories, we cultivate our imaginations and create memories that outlive us. As our kids grew, Gabe and I encouraged them to create their own memories. We taught them to see that with a little imagination, nothing was impossible or off-limits, and now they're using their imaginations to create blessings for others, including Gabe and me. Pierce wrote a song for my fortieth birthday. Kennedy painted watercolors to give to family and friends.

WHEN WE MAKE MEMORIES, WE CULTIVATE OUR IMAGINATIONS AND CREATE MEMORIES THAT OUTLIVE US.

Making memories and using our imaginations requires us to show up, which is next to impossible when you're mired in burnout, depression, and anxiety. So the next time you find yourself at the end of a difficult week, instead of disengaging or escaping, what if you made a memory? What if you completed some kind of family project or made a family film? What if you baked Christmas cookies in July or created a silly new game? Making memories helps us step outside ourselves, even if just for a moment. In seasons of great stress or anxiety, it might be the very thing that turns everything around.

⇗ REFLECTION QUESTIONS ⇖

1. REFLECT ON YOUR ACTIVITIES OVER THE LAST FEW MONTHS. ARE YOU MAKING CREATIVE, IMAGINATIVE MEMORIES WITH YOUR FAMILY OR FRIENDS? IF NOT, WHAT ARE SOME CHANGES YOU COULD MAKE TO ENSURE YOU NURTURE IMAGINATION AND PLAY, IN YOURSELF AND IN YOUR FAMILY AND FRIENDS?

2. WHAT ARE SOME OF THE CREATIVE THINGS YOU HAVE DONE WITH FAMILY OR FRIENDS THAT HAVE BECOME LASTING MEMORIES? WHAT ABOUT THOSE EXPERIENCES MADE THEM SO MEMORABLE?

3. CARVE OUT TIME THIS FRIDAY OR SATURDAY NIGHT. SIT AROUND THE TABLE AND ASK YOUR FAMILY, "HOW CAN WE MAKE A CREATIVE, LASTING MEMORY?" SEE IF THE CONVERSATION DOESN'T DEVELOP INTO HILARITY.

TAKE
CARE OF
SOMETHING

CHAPTER 27

CHAPTER 27

TAKE CARE OF SOMETHING

BE RESPONSIBLE

In dreams begin responsibilities.

—W. B. YEATS

We were returning from our annual retreat—the one where Gabe and I spend a few days alone, *sans* children, forgetting anything that reminds us of our frenetic lives. Every year as we're heading back home, we recommit to doing it again the next year, knowing these times away are essential to keeping the chemistry alive.

As we walked up to the door to greet our children, something in the left corner of my vision grabbed my attention. I looked down and saw white feathers strewn everywhere, as if a down pillow had exploded over the bushes and our stone path. Clearly, we'd just stepped into a fresh and savage crime scene. The victim: one of our five-month-old chickens. As I followed the feather trail into the woods, I knew we were lucky only one of our dozen had become a feast for the raccoon family camping in our woods.

As I glanced over to the coop, the door appeared to be unlatched and hanging open.

Now, there aren't many animals cuter than yellow, fluffy, baby chickens. Until this year, I'd only observed these cuties on the web or in a children's petting zoo. But that all changed when Kennedy decided she wanted to participate in our county's 4H project. The project? Raise a dozen hens from birth to six months old, then auction off five at the county fair. The payoff? We keep a few hens and eat lots of omelets, scrambled eggs, and breakfasts for dinner!

There was a bigger reason we said yes to chickens, though, and it had nothing to do with eggs. It had to do with anxiety. Not mine, but Kennedy's.

Her experience as a seventh grader brought a lot of unexpected twists. Midway through the year, she began feeling shortness of breath, fear, and a mild form of panic attacks. I'd been through this in my late thirties, but my daughter? At age twelve? Was it possible?

While Kennedy wasn't eager to take on a little added responsibility, we thought it might help her turn the corner. Let me explain why.

INSTILLING THE CONFIDENCE THAT OVERCOMES ANXIETY

Kennedy is not alone in her anxiety. *The Washington Post* reported, "Anxiety, not depression, is the leading mental health issue among American youths."[1] Philip Kendall, director of the Child and

Adolescent Anxiety Disorders Clinic at Temple University and a practicing psychologist, explains teens are "growing up in an environment of volatility, where schools have lockdowns, where there are wars across borders. We used to have high confidence in our environment—now we have an environment that anticipates catastrophe."[2]

ACCORDING TO THE NATIONAL INSTITUTES OF HEALTH, ALMOST A THIRD OF ALL ADOLESCENTS WILL EXPERIENCE AN ANXIETY DISORDER DURING THEIR LIFETIME.

It makes sense. Many adults can't handle the volume of information, violence, disagreement, breaking news, social media flare-ups, and noise, so how could a child? It's all just too much. According to the National Institutes of Health, almost a third of all adolescents will experience an anxiety disorder during their lifetime, and girls suffer most, with incidences as high as 38 percent, with boys at 26 percent.[3]

This leads me back to Viktor Frankl's ideas that *unfulfilled responsibility* leads to feelings of anxiety. Could this be why so many of our young are floundering with their feelings?

In a study surveying recent decades, the data shows that teenagers are not preparing for adulthood responsibilities like they once did. Among twelfth graders, there is a steep decline in behaviors over the last twenty-five years that prove the point, including: 55 percent worked for pay, down from 76 percent; and 73 percent have drivers' licenses, down from 88 percent.[4]

These statistics make it clear: there is a significant decline in teenage responsibility. Combine this with their increased access to adult information and their waning sense of safety, and it's not hard to see how overwhelming this world can feel at times.

GROWING CHICKENS, GROWING CONFIDENCE

Moms and dads, don't let your guard down. We must be vigilant to keep our children's minds from being paralyzed by fear, and vigilant is what Gabe and I were. We crafted a strategy for Kennedy to beat back feelings of anxiety when they spring up, a strategy that's grown from my own practices. We taught our daughter to pray Scripture out loud during her darkest moments, and she's been consistent with the practice. It's helped her overcome her momentary anxious feelings. Still, Gabe and I knew there must be more we could do to help her. So we started asking the bigger question—even of our twelve-year-old: what *unfulfilled responsibilities* exist in her life, even subconsciously?

We began to ask whether Kennedy had any real responsibilities, whether she knew she was needed and counted on. So when she decided she wanted to tackle an optional 4H project, we seized the opportunity, knowing that seeing her purpose in the caregiving and nurturing of vulnerable animals might fill her with a sense of responsibility. She'd have to raise baby chicks into full-fledged mamas. She'd have to work through the daily, mundane activities of feeding and watering these cute little critters and harvesting eggs in order to succeed. And if she didn't play her part, those chicks would suffer.

The night we discovered feathers everywhere, Kennedy had failed in one of her responsibilities. It was easy to understand; the thunderstorm that wreaked havoc an hour earlier coincided with the time she typically locks the chicken coop. But after the storm passed, she'd forgotten, and so, when we told her about the missing chicken, she was shocked.

"Mom, how could that have happened? It was only thirty minutes ago that it stopped raining, and I was planning to go back out, but I forgot."

I replied, "It's okay, honey. We are just glad the raccoon only got one. These chickens can't defend themselves; they are counting on you for their protection. Let's make sure it doesn't happen again."

With tears in her eyes, she said, "I'm sorry. I feel so bad for that chicken." We reassured her again, told her this is just how the circle of life goes sometimes, and then we engaged in that same circle of life.

Weeks later Kennedy bathed the remaining chickens' feet, fluffed their feathers, and entered her five best chickens in the Williamson County Fair. When we arrived that night after the judging was complete, we were filled with excitement. And when we got to Kennedy's exhibit, we saw a blue ribbon atop her pen. First prize! Blue ribbon chickens for Kennedy Lyons!

The responsibility of caring for and protecting those chickens boosted Kennedy's confidence. She knew she'd been given a task, worked hard to carry it out, and succeeded. In the days afterward, I sensed a shift in her demeanor. Anxiousness was giving way to a newfound confidence as she continued to pursue new areas of responsibility in the weeks and months that followed.

WHAT'S GOOD FOR THE CHICKS IS GOOD FOR THE HEN

What's true for Kennedy is true for all of us. Sure, I've had plenty of days when I just wanted to curl up on the couch, blanket pulled over my eyes, and nap the day away. In the moment, that can seem like the best thing to do for myself. But a few days in a row like that leads me straight into a deeper depression, one wherein I just don't want to do anything.

How do I break the cycle? I take on responsibilities that inspire me to get out of bed and out the door, to show up. Whether it's weekly meetings with my team at work, or lunch dates with one of our kids who needs advice, or agreeing to a book deadline or speaking engagement, I say yes when the right opportunities for responsibility present themselves. Having obligations and responsibilities reminds me I'm needed, that I have a critical role to play—and knowing this balances out my mental health.

When I have responsibilities, when folks are relying on me, I come alive. I feel purposeful. I feel engaged. I feel needed.

———

WHEN WE ARE RESPONSIBLE FOR DOING CERTAIN THINGS, IT MAKES US FEEL NEEDED AND USEFUL. WHEN WE SUCCEED, WE'RE FILLED WITH NEW CONFIDENCE.

———

Though you can't work your way out of anxiety or depression (in fact, you can overwork your way into it), creating the conditions for sustained mental and emotional health requires creating moments of responsibility in your life. When we are responsible for doing certain things, it makes us feel needed and useful. When we succeed, we're filled with new confidence. If you're stuck in a rut of anxiety, see whether there's some unexplored opportunity for responsibility in your life.

⟋ REFLECTION QUESTIONS ⟍

1. WHAT RESPONSIBILITIES MOTIVATE YOU?

2. LIST THE MEANING BEHIND EACH OF THE RESPONSIBILITIES NOTED ABOVE. HOW CAN YOU MAXIMIZE THAT PURPOSE AND MEANING?

3. WHAT NEW AREAS OF RESPONSIBILITY CAN YOU PUSH INTO, AREAS THAT MIGHT GIVE YOU A SENSE OF ACCOMPLISHMENT, CONFIDENCE, AND JOY?

SAY YES

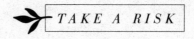

TAKE A RISK

CHAPTER 28

SAY YES

TAKE A RISK

Security is mostly a superstition . . . Life is either a daring adventure or nothing.

—HELEN KELLER

Each time I was pregnant, Gabe and I snuck away for a baby-moon. We made it a priority so we could reconnect before the chaos set in. We'd drop off whatever kids we had at "Camp Meeme and Papa" and hide away somewhere tropical. Why I agreed to wear a swimsuit six months into each pregnancy, I'll never know. But lounging poolside with endless chips and guacamole, talking with Gabe, and reading books and magazines was a good way to recharge for the coming season.

During our third babymoon, when I was pregnant with Kennedy, I stood on the edge of the pool, ready to jump in, and said to Gabe,

"Babe, this will be my third C-section. I can't imagine having the physical or emotional capacity for more children after this." My doctor had cautioned us about the amount of scar tissue building up when Pierce was born and had growing concerns that my uterus might rupture if I went into labor. Not only that but Cade had yet to poop in the potty at age five. I imagined a life of changing diapers forever, and it was overwhelming. I suppose that's why I said, "If it's a girl, I want to get my tubes tied." Gabe responded, "Only if you're open to adoption." It was an out-of-the-blue comment, and of course I said I was open to it if that meant I could get off the child-bearing merry-go-round. What did "open" mean, anyway? Three months later, after tugging and loud cries in the operating room, Gabe cried out, "It's a GIRL!" to which I responded, "Tie me up."

Two years later, I heard a message about how children were a blessing, which I already knew, but the truth of what I had done set in with a new sort of conviction. I marched back into my ob-gyn office asking if Mr. Ob-gyn doctor could undo the thing I had begged for two years prior. He, of course, explained in his rational, steady voice that un-tying my tubes would be a fourth incision in the same spot as the first three. If I ended up pregnant, that would be a fifth surgery in the exact same place. For liability reasons and for my safety, he wasn't willing to do it.

This is where I pause to say I regret tying my tubes at age thirty-one. This isn't a prescriptive statement, just an honest one. Thinking of the many women I know who are trying everything to have children, it feels cavalier, like I played God with something permanent, determining when we should be done having kids simply because I was tired. Now hear me clearly: I'm not questioning the wisdom of family planning, but for me, something less permanent would have been wiser. If I'd just given myself a few more years, a little distance from the operating room, it would have offered a better vantage point. Still, the silver lining of all this was Gabe's knee-jerk invitation to consider a future adoption.

The adoption conversation surfaced for about thirty minutes every three years after my doctor's appointment, and though many of our friends were adopting, we never quite felt the timing was right. We were three steps behind sanity, barely keeping our heads above water on the parenting front. Of course, much of this was our own fault. We were maxed out, always on the move, and doing our best to live and work in a two-bedroom apartment. So our conversations about adoption were few and fleeting, but we still had them.

When we moved to Tennessee, our kids were ten, twelve, and fourteen. We considered adoption again, this time feeling a little more margin in our lives to entertain the possibility. Still, we weren't ready. Bringing a baby into our family as our kids were about to move into middle and high school felt ambitious. Conventional wisdom said our lives were too busy with good things, and we needed to focus on our current kids and on what we were already committed to without piling on more. So we kept kicking the conversation down the road.

Meanwhile, Kennedy had dreams of her own. She'd imagined she'd have a baby sister, and she wasn't shy about asking for one. She didn't just ask, though. She prayed and prayed for a baby sister. In fact, she had since she was five.

One night, our family went to see *War Room*, a movie with a character who prayed faithfully in her closet—the war room—for years, and saw her prayers answered. Later that night, I walked into

Kennedy's room to find her washi-taping a series of written prayers up and down the walls of her closet. One asked God to help our family adopt. Time and time again, we downplayed the odds that it would happen, hoping this would let Kennedy down without hurting her. Yet she never gave up. In fact, she was so persistent that Gabe sat her down and suggested her passion for adoption was God preparing her to adopt a child one day in her adult life, because it wasn't likely we would. Weeks after that conversation, I saw that particular prayer torn in two, one-half of it hanging from the wall by a piece of tape. When I asked Kennedy about it, she looked down at the ground and said, "I figure it's never going to happen."

Kennedy's prayers must have worked over time, though, because one day I surrendered it all. *If this is something you want to happen*, I prayed, *please bring her to me. Please put her right in front of my face, and I'll name her Joy.*

Three years later, on December 3, 2018, my dear friend Meredith in Beijing, China, texted me a photo of an adorable five-year-old grinning ear to ear, a child with Down syndrome. Meredith wrote, "This girl's file is going to the US tomorrow." The message was totally unexpected. I thought, *Why is she doing this to me?* (Meredith has a particular knack for persuasion.)

I responded, "She's adorable. What's her name?

"Chara," she replied.

I gasped. "You mean the Greek word for *joy*?"

When I got Meredith's text, I wanted to run. We were days from celebrating twenty years of marriage, and visions of growing independence danced in my head. I remember telling Gabe, full of fear, "This feels like the day I got Cade's diagnosis. The day everything changed for our future, and we started a life different than what we imagined."

Gabe listened. Let me say my piece. I continued.

"But it's not that scary because we'll never be empty nesters anyway," I said. I pictured the bond that would form between Cade and Joy, buddies for a good long while after the other two went to college and started independent lives.

Then it hit me. "Perhaps God gave us Cade because he knew seventeen years later he'd give us Joy, and we'd say 'yes.'" Gabe held me while I cried tears of surrender. This was indeed an invitation into something more. Instead of being empty nesters in five years, we'd be heading back to kindergarten.

PARTNERING IN GOD'S CREATION

Taking a risk may be the hardest thing you'll ever do, but it's the only way we can partner with God in creating good and beautiful things. Some risks are smaller, like hopping a plane across the country— while others are larger, like adopting a baby from across the world. Giving up control of the routine, our norms, and our comforts and moving into the unknown is paralyzing. Especially as we age.

TAKING A RISK MAY BE THE HARDEST THING YOU'LL EVER DO, BUT IT'S THE ONLY WAY WE CAN PARTNER WITH GOD IN CREATING GOOD AND BEAUTIFUL THINGS.

Research shows that as we get older, our dopamine levels decrease, making us more adverse to risky behavior.[1] This can be a good thing, helping us avoid dangerous activities that could lead to injury. But it might also mean remaining on the sidelines when adventure awaits. Taking risks assumes a reward or failure. That's just part of the dynamic. But when we stop allowing ourselves to dream, or decide we want to be comfortable and conservative, we just may be missing out on a way to partner with God, and as we partner with him in creating a life of faith, we'll learn to "not worry about tomorrow, for tomorrow will worry about itself."[2] We'll learn to live in the peace and joy of God's purpose for us.

The call and assignment of God is never possible without God.

THE CALL AND ASSIGNMENT OF GOD IS NEVER POSSIBLE WITHOUT GOD.

As I write this, it's the first week of December—exactly one year after Meredith sent that life-changing text—a text that came *two weeks after* God gave me the word "abundance" for the coming season, and now we're at the end of the adoption process. We're in Guangxi, China, and tomorrow is "Gotcha Day," the day our daughter, Joy Lyons, will join our family forever. The adoption agency will bring her in with no pomp, circumstance, or fanfare, and in minutes they'll place her in my arms. We'll have twenty-four hours to decide if we want to keep her (yes, this is a thing) then come back to sign papers, dip our thumbs in red ink, and seal the moment.

Joy's new middle name on the documents will be Levi, my daddy's middle name. When he died in April, I was afraid to proceed with adopting Joy, consumed by the fear of risking it all, overtaken by grief. I considered the option of running, but we were well underway. One morning I woke early and heard a whisper: *Fight death with life.*

It's so like the enemy, after a long stretch of faith, to threaten obedience with fear. But this risk ends in beauty, the culmination of partnering with God to create a new reality for our family. This year of surrendered prayers and tears called our family to a singular focus, to prepare our hearts and home for God's glorious interruption.

And though I should be nervous, anxious, maybe even a bit panicky, I'm not. Why? Because Advent is the culmination of a sacred waiting for new life to come. It requires constant trust and yielding to a plan beyond our own. Tomorrow we enter God's story for Joy, and we couldn't be more grateful.

Is there a risk you've been avoiding, something you know God might be calling you to do? If you're not following through, not taking the risk, it might be leading to anxiety, stress, or depression. Determine the risk you might need to take, and take the leap. In it, you might find unexpected joy.

⟋ REFLECTION QUESTIONS ⟍

1. LIST THE WAYS YOU MIGHT TAKE A RISK TO PARTNER WITH GOD. IS THERE A RISK YOU KNOW YOU NEED TO ACT ON IMMEDIATELY?

2. HAS GOD ASKED YOU TO TAKE A RISK THAT YOU ARE NOT WILLING TO TAKE? WHY ARE YOU SO CLOSED TO IT?

3. TO TAKE A HOLY RISK, WE HAVE TO TRUST THAT GOD HAS A SPECIFIC PURPOSE FOR OUR LIVES. WHAT DOES THAT STATEMENT MEAN TO YOU?

YOU
WERE
MADE
FOR
THIS

 *CONCLUSION*

YOU WERE MADE FOR THIS

The more that you read, the more things you will know. The more that you learn, the more places you'll go.

—DR. SEUSS

What terrified me most about adopting a five-year-old was the possibility that I wouldn't be up for it. I worried that every natural mama-to-toddler instinct had gone down the drain years ago, and I'd be a train wreck by naptime each day. But now that Joy is home, I realize those worries were just my anxiety talking. In fact, I'm shocked at how much I love being her mom. Perhaps because I'd prepared myself for the worst (adoption videos do an excellent job of this), while we still knew it was the right decision, this fear surfaced for the better part of twelve months.

Day one was harder than I thought, day three more magical than I could've imagined. Each moment with this curious girl inspires me to stay young, to muster the same energy I had in my twenties. She wakes each morning with the happiest smile and loves FaceTime and her baby doll and blow dryers and running. I can't imagine the shift in her little heart, but her silent tears as she was leaving the orphanage she called "home" have been traded for silliness and laughter. (She is a regular laugh box. Never in my life have I felt so funny.)

Two months on the other side of Gotcha Day, priorities have shifted and made room for Joy's beautiful interruption to our lives. I still have my old mothering instincts—when to take Joy to the potty, when to read a pile of board books, when to just sit and sing "Skinnamarink" together—and my heart is so full of light.

I'm in awe of the wonder of adoption. How a brave birth mama chose life and hope and let another raise her daughter. How we can fly to the other side of the world, where a girl is waiting for her forever family. How we can fly with her for thirty hours and put her in the open arms of her big sister and brothers back home. How an entire community can show up at the Nashville airport at midnight with banners and bubbles to welcome her for the happiest homecoming.

Joy-girl, these are the ones who loved you long before they knew you. Who prayed and hoped and encouraged. The sweetest people, ready to embrace you with open arms.

This adventure has been more than I could've asked for. When God gave me the word ***abundance*** at the beginning of the year, this is exactly what he meant. But would I have been able to receive it if I'd been stuck in an endless cycle of anxiety and panic? Would I have had the imagination for such a major shift in my life? Or would I have seen it as something impossible?

Maybe you feel the tug toward something (anything) that feels impossible. Maybe you feel called to something that is beyond your reach because you are so full of anxiety, worry, or panic. Take heart. God gently beckons, never coerces, and offers the grace to fall into rhythms that will fill you with confidence and courage, confirm your calling, and give you strength to carry out his purposes. But this confidence, courage, and strength isn't what the world teaches. There's nothing more beautiful than finding strength on the other side of yes. It's not a strength of doing, but one of being. Being in the center of his will.

Our society is relentless. It's a nonstop, ever-churning, production-oriented, get-stuff-done society. If we're not careful, it can get the best of all of us. The Scriptures give us clear direction, though: "Do not conform to the pattern of this world, but be transformed by the renewing of your mind. Then you will be able to test and approve what God's will is—his good, pleasing and perfect will."[1] It's the renewing of our minds, then, that brings the transformation of our imaginations, that pulls us from the world's restless cycle. When we live into this renewal, we'll find our stress and anxiety transformed into peace and purpose. We'll find ourselves living in the center of God's will. We'll find ourselves with the strength and courage to do the unimaginable.

THE RHYTHMS OF LIVING

Over the years, I've come to see just how important the four rhythms we've explored in this book are to my emotional, relational, physical, and spiritual health. These rhythms not only protect me from anxiety and the stress of the world. They are the very thing that helped me come alive, engaged with vision that allowed me to see the path to Joy. Granted, I'm not always the best practitioner, and there are plenty of times when I drop the ball. When I do, you can be sure I slip right back into my old need to strive and keep up, and the old feelings of panic sneak back in. When those first hints of a meltdown come calling, I return to the rhythms of renewal God has given us—Rest, Restoration, Connection, and Creation—and find the deep peace and purpose he's created me to experience.

As you've journeyed through this book with me, you've likely identified areas where you come up short. Maybe you can't seem to slow down, can't seem to rest. Maybe you don't take time to engage in restorative practices or can't seem to connect with anyone. Perhaps you've lost the desire to create anything. That's okay. None of us are perfect. Note those rhythms of renewal that will take more work for you, and make a plan to intentionally incorporate them into your daily life. As you do, as you combine them with the rhythms that might come more naturally, you'll experience a deeper sense of calm and peace in the presence of God. You'll begin to see purpose you never thought possible.

None of this will be easy, but make it your goal. Mix and match the rhythms. Be relentless in your pursuit of them so that you can look back at your calendar each week and see the ways you've rested, found restoration, connected, and created something with God. If you practice these habits consistently, I know you'll find the renewed mind and the transformed life you so desire.

LET'S CULTIVATE THE VIBRANT LIFE
WE WERE MEANT TO LIVE.

Let's do this together, shall we?

Let's live into these blessed rhythms to Rest, Restore, Connect, and Create. Let's quiet inner chaos and make room for flourishing. Let's establish daily habits that keep us mentally and physically strong.

When we do, we cultivate the vibrant life we were meant to live. We take charge of our emotional health and inspire our loved ones to do the same. We find joy through restored relationships in our families and communities.

If we partner together, we can make a difference in the world around us. We can walk in confidence as we offer our unique gifts to one another. We can become the carriers of peace our world longs to see.

ACKNOWLEDGMENTS

To the Lyons, DeWeese and Scarberry families; your love and encouragement throughout my life keeps me dreaming, writing, and believing in God's goodness. Thank you, forever and always, for being my household of faith.

To the lifelong friends who've become family, you are grounding for me: Wendy White, Heather Larson, Shannon Mescher, Trina McNeilly, Christy Nockels, Lauren Tomlin, Amber Haines, Lori and Tori Benham, and Ann Voskamp. You've walked alongside me through hills and valleys, and I'm forever blessed by your persistent presence.

To generous friends who championed and believed in this message: Elisabeth Hasselbeck, Bob Goff, Lysa TerKeurst, Sadie Robertson, Curt Thompson, Candace Cameron Bure, John Townsend, Alena Pitts, Banning Liebscher, Lisa Bevere, and Jon Tyson.

To my agent and longtime friend Chris Ferebee, for your discernment and wisdom; to Dana Tanamachi, for your beautiful artwork adorning the cover; and to Aaron Campbell, for your meticulous design throughout these pages, thank you for lending your creativity to this book. To Carolyn McCready, Seth Haines, Liz Heaney, and Harmony Harkema, you are the best editorial team a girl could dream of! You kept pressing and tweaking and persisting. Your talents grow mine tremendously!

To David Morris, Brandon Henderson, Tom Dean, Robin Barnett, Curt Diepenhorst, and the rest of the Zondervan team, thank you for cheering loud and believing in this message, I am deeply grateful. To Abby Coutant, Emily Pastina, Kellie Ritcher, Katy Boatman, and Caleb Peavy for your brilliant support. It's my honor to collaborate and create with you!

In closing with my people; to Gabe, Cade, Pierce, Kennedy and Joy. Each day I wake to watch you grow in love for God and each other. There is no greater treasure for the heart of a wife and mama. When the lights fade and the silence settles, you will always be *home*, the ones my heart longs for. God has granted each of you as a gift to show me more of him. I love you forever.

NOTES

INTRODUCTION

1. 1 Cor. 10:13, paraphrase mine.
2. "What Is Stress," The American Institute of Stress, https://www.stress.org/daily-life.
3. "The Source of Your Stress," Forbes Magazine (website) https://www.forbes.com/sites/cywakeman/2013/06/20/the-source-of-your-stress/#4999f9c97626.
4. Borwin Bandelow and Sophie Michaelis, "Epidemiology of Anxiety Disorders in the 20th Century," *Dialogues in Clinical Neuroscience* 17 no. 3 (September 2015): 327–335, https://www.ncbi.nlm.nih.gov/pmc/articles/PMC4610617/.
5. "Depression," National Alliance on Mental Illness, https://www.nami.org/Learn-More/Mental-Health-Conditions/Depression.
6. John 14:27 (NLT).
7. Matthew Pryor, "The Most Frequent Command in the Bible," Crosswalk, May 3, 2016, https://www.crosswalk.com/faith/bible-study/the-most-frequent-command-in-the-bible.html.

RHYTHM 1: REST

1. Genesis 2:2–3.
2. Leviticus 26:6.
3. Leviticus 26:3–4.
4. Leviticus 26:9.

CHAPTER 1

1. Parker J. Palmer, *Let Your Life Speak* (San Francisco, CA: Jossey-Bass, 2009), 1.
2. Romans 14:12.
3. Psalm 139:16.
4. Ephesians 3:20.

CHAPTER 2

1. Galatians 1:10 ESV.

CHAPTER 3

1. Susan Cain, *Quiet: The Power of Introverts in a World That Can't Stop Talking* (New York, NY: Crown Publishers, 2012), 11.
2. Travis Bradbury, "9 Signs that You're an Ambivert," *Forbes* (April 26, 2016) https://www.forbes.com/sites/travisbradberry/2016/04/26/9-signs-that-youre-an-ambivert/#4c2ff7493145.
3. Amy Morin, "7 Science-Backed Reasons You Should Spend More Time Alone," *Forbes* (August 5, 2017) https://www.forbes.com/sites/amymorin/2017/08/05/7-science-backed-reasons-you-should-spend-more-time-alone/#4859cdf61b7e.
4. Author Emerson Eggerichs stated this to Gabe and me when we spent time with him in marriage counseling. He said most people think the key to a great marriage is "good communication," but this is false. The key to a great marriage is mutual understanding.

CHAPTER 4

1. James 5:16; Ephesians 5:13.
2. Romans 8:28.
3. Proverbs 4:23.

CHAPTER 5

1. "Consequences of Insufficient Sleep," Healthy Sleep, http://healthysleep.med.harvard.edu/healthy/matters/consequences.
2. Arianna Huffington, *The Sleep Revolution: Transforming Your Life, One Night at a Time* (New York, NY: Penguin Random House, 2016), 28.
3. Ibid., 40.

CHAPTER 6

1. Douglas Kaine McKelvey, *Every Moment Holy* (Nashville, TN: Rabbit Room Press, 2017), 135.
2. Philippians 4:6–7.

CHAPTER 7

1. Isaiah 58:13–14 MSG.
2. Genesis 2:2–3.

3. Timothy Baron, "What Is Fallow Ground?" Hunker, https://www
.hunker.com/13428082/what-is-fallow-ground.
4. Eugene Peterson was interviewed by my husband, Gabe Lyons, for a
Q Session event on "Practices" at the Crosby Hotel in New York City
during the winter of 2013. He spent an hour describing his Sabbath
practice to the audience of 100, and this was one of the rhythms he
emphasized.

RHYTHM 2: RESTORE
1. "Restore," *Dictionary.com*, https://www.dictionary.com/browse/
restore.

CHAPTER 8
1. Jennifer Wallace, "Why It's Good for Grown-ups to Go Play,"
Washington Post (May 20, 2017) https://www.washingtonpost
.com/national/health-science/why-its-good-for-grown-ups-to-go
-play/2017/05/19/99810292-fd1f-11e6-8ebe-6e0dbe4f2bca_story.
html?utm_term=.a92aaa19d812.
2. Cale D. Magnuson and Lynn Barnett, *The Playful Advantage: How
Playfulness Enhances Coping with Stress* (Milton Park, Abingdon: Leisure
Sciences, 2013) 35, 129–144.
3. Ibid.

CHAPTER 9
1. Eva Selhub, M.D.; "Nutritional Psychiatry: Your Brain on Food,"
Harvard Health Blog (Nov. 16, 2015) https://www.health.harvard.
edu/blog/nutritional-psychiatry-your-brain-on-food-201511168626.
2. Ibid.
3. Adrienne O'Neil, Shae E. Quirk, Siobhan Housden, Sharon L.
Brennan, Lana J. Williams, Julie A. Pasco, Michael Berk, and Felice N.
Jacka, "Relationship Between Diet and Mental Health in Children and
Adolescents: A Systematic Review" (October 2014) Am J Public Heal,
https://www.ncbi.nlm.nih.gov/pmc/articles/PMC4167107/.

CHAPTER 10
1. Psalm 139:13–14

2. David Kinnaman and Gabe Lyons, *Good Faith: Being a Christian When Society Thinks You're Irrelevant and Extreme* (Grand Rapids, MI: Baker Books, 2016), 34.

CHAPTER 11

1. "Seasonal Affective Disorder," National Institute of Mental Health, https://www.nimh.nih.gov/health/topics/seasonal-affective-disorder/index.shtml.
2. Nilofer Merchant, "Sitting Is the Smoking of Our Generation," *Harvard Business Review* (January 14, 2013) https://hbr.org/2013/01/sitting-is-the-smoking-of-our-generation.
3. Jessica Gross, "Walking Meetings? 5 Surprising Thinkers Who Swore by Them, TEDblog (April 29, 2013) https://blog.ted.com/walking-meetings-5-surprising-thinkers-who-swore-by-them/.

CHAPTER 12

1. Gregory Berns, *Iconoclast: A Neuroscientist Reveals How to Think Differently*, (Brighton, MA: Harvard Business Press, 2010), 81.
2. Ibid., 8.

CHAPTER 13

1. "Water and Green Spaces" *The Telegraph* (May 6, 2019) https://www.telegraph.co.uk/health-fitness/mind/water-green-spaces-calm-mind-bank-holiday/.
2. Learn more about this bike at Mobocruiser.com.
3. Ashish Sharma, M.D.; Vishal Madaan, M.D.; and Frederick D. Petty, M.D., Ph.D.; "Exercise for Mental Health," The Primary Care Companion to the Journal of Clinical Psychiatry 8 no. 2 (2006): 106, https://www.ncbi.nlm.nih.gov/pmc/articles/PMC1470658/.
4. A. Davis, C. Valsecchi, and M. Fergusson, *Unfit for Purpose: How Car Use Fuels Climate Change and Obesity* (London: IEEP, 2007) 12.
5. WHO. World Health Report; World Health Organisation: Geneva, 2004.
6. P. Ekkekakis, E.E. Hall, L.M. Van Landuyt & S. Petruzzello, "Walking In (Affective) Circles: Can Short Walks Enhance Affect?" *Journal of Behavioral Medicine* 23 no. 3 (June 2000): 245–275.

7. Jo Borton and Jules Pretty, "What Is the Best Dose of Nature and Green Exercise for Improving Mental Health? A Multi-Study Analysis," https://texanbynature.org/wp-content/uploads/2016/10/ What-is-the-Best-Dose-of-Nature-and-Gre . . . -Mental-Health-A -Multi-Study-Analysis.pdf

CHAPTER 14

1. Rochelle Perper, Ph.D., "The Psychological Benefits of Risk Taking," Therapy Changes (June 23, 2014) https://therapychanges.com/ blog/2014/06/psychological-benefits-risk/.

CHAPTER 15

1. See https://www.amazon.com/Nicomachean-Ethics-Oxford -Worlds-Classics/dp/0199213615/ref=pd_sbs_14_t_0?_encoding =UTF8&psc=1&refRID=C4E9BCFS8GM5VJP33GTB.
2. Ibid.
3. Quoted in Brad Stulberg, "The Incredible Power of Friendship," Medium.com (Jan. 12, 2018) https://medium.com/personal-growth/ the-incredible-power-of-friendship-b061833959c2.

CHAPTER 16

1. Brené Brown, *Daring Greatly: How the Courage to Be Vulnerable Transforms the Way We Live, Love, Parent, and Lead* (New York, NY: Penguin Publishing Group, 2015) page 34.
2. Quoted in Daniel Coyle, "How Showing Vulnerability Helps Build a Stronger Team," Ideas.Ted.Com (Feb. 20, 2018) https://ideas.ted.com/ how-showing-vulnerability-helps-build-a-stronger-team/.
3. Ibid.
4. At a retreat I attended where Dr. John Townsend was speaking, he shared this anecdote, which I found to be helpful.

CHAPTER 17

1. D'vera Cohn and Rich Morin, "Who Moves? Who Stays Put? Where's Home? *Pew Research Center*, http://www.pewsocialtrends .org/2008/12/17/who-moves-who-stays-put-wheres-home/ (Dec. 17, 2008).

2. Linda Poon, "Why Won't You Be My Neighbor?" *CityLab*, https://www.citylab.com/equity/2015/08/why-wont-you-be-my-neighbor/401762/ (Aug. 19, 2015).

CHAPTER 18

1. "Tear Bottle History," Lachrymatory.com, http://www.lachrymatory.com/History.htm.

2. Luke 7:48

3. Asmir Gracanin, Lauren M. Bylsma, and Ad J. J. M. Vingerhoets, "Is Crying a Self-soothing Behavior?" Frontiers in Psychology, https://www.ncbi.nlm.nih.gov/pmc/articles/PMC4035568/ (May 28, 2014).

4. Lizette Borreli, "Cry It Out: 6 Surprising Health Benefits of Shedding a Few Tears," Medical Daily, https://www.medicaldaily.com/cry-it-out-6-surprising-health-benefits-shedding-few-tears-333952 (May 19, 2015).

5. Galatians 6:2 NLT

6. Frank T. McAndrew, Ph.D., "The Perils of Social Isolation," Psychology Today Blog, https://www.psychologytoday.com/us/blog/out-the-ooze/201611/the-perils-social-isolation (Nov. 12, 2016).

7. Emily Sohn, "More and More Research Shows Friends Are Good for Your Health," *Washington Post*, https://www.washingtonpost.com/national/health-science/more-and-more-research-shows-friends-are-good-for-your-health/2016/05/26/f249e754-204d-11e6-9e7f-57890b612299_story.html?utm_term=.896b0e3d1600 (, May 26, 2016).

CHAPTER 19

1. "The Benefits of Hugging," SiOWfa15: Science in Our World: Certainty and Controversy, https://sites.psu.edu/siowfa15/2015/09/18/the-benefits-of-hugging/.

2. Jennifer Miller, "20 Amazing Benefits of Hugging According to Science," GenerationNext.com, https://www.generationnext.com.au/2017/05/20-amazing-benefits-hugging-according-science/ (May 22, 2017).

3. Sabrina Barr, "Why Are Most Babies Conceived Around Christmas?" *The Independent*, https://www.independent.co.uk/life-style/

health-and-families/babies-conceive-christmas-why-most-parents
-couples-conception-a8103201.html (Dec. 11, 2017).

4. Benedict Carey, "Evidence That Little Touches Do Mean So Much," *The New York Times*, https://www.nytimes.com/2010/02/23/health/23mind.html?scp=3&sq=touch&st=cse (Feb. 22, 2010).

5. Ibid.

6. Mark 8:25

7. Luke 4:40

8. Luke 13:12–13.

9. Luke 18:15–17.

10. Luke 7:45

11. Luke 7:47

CHAPTER 20

1. First, Emerson's approach is based on Ephesians 5:33, "However, each one of you also must love his wife as he loves himself, and the wife must respect her husband" (NIV). This wasn't Emerson's theory but his quoting the summary to the greatest treatise on marriage in the New Testament. Second, yes, wives need respect and honor (1 Peter 3:7) and husbands need love (Titus 2:4) but most commonly the felt need during conflict is that a wife feels unloved and a husband feels disrespected. Emerson pointed out his research among 7,000 married people. He asked them, "When in a conflict, do you feel unloved or disrespected at that moment?" Eighty-three percent of the husbands said they felt disrespected, and 72% of the wives felt unloved. In Emerson's book, *Love and Respect* he explores in-depth what this looks like, and it certainly does not mean we love and respect bad behavior.

2. "Marriage Helps Cancer Survival," *The Telegraph*, April 11, 2016, https://www.telegraph.co.uk/news/2016/04/11/marriage-helps-cancer-survival/.

3. Jonathan Wells, "Marriage Makes You Stronger-and Eight Other Health Benefits of Tying the Knot," *The Telegraph*, https://www.telegraph.co.uk/health-fitness/body/the-eight-surprising-health-benefits-of-getting-married/ (Jan. 24, 2019).

CHAPTER 21

1. Ephesians 4:26–27
2. "Foothold," Cambridge Dictionary, https://dictionary.cambridge.org/us/dictionary/english/foothold.
3. John 10:10
4. "Forgiveness: Your Health Depends On It," Johns Hopkins Medicine, https://www.hopkinsmedicine.org/health/healthy_aging/healthy_connections/forgiveness-your-health-depends-on-it.

RHYTHM 4: CREATE

1. Genesis 2:15.
2. Ephesians 2:10.

CHAPTER 22

1. Viktor Frankl, *Man's Search for Meaning*, (Boston, MA: Beacon Press, 1959), 165.
2. Galatians 5:14 MSG.
3. Frankl, 132.
4. Rakesh Kochhar, "How Americans Compare to the Global Middle Class," Pew Research Center, http://www.pewresearch.org/fact-tank/2015/07/09/how-americans-compare-with-the-global-middle-class/ (July 9, 2015).
5. Diana Divecha and Robin Stern, "American Teens Are Stressed and Bored. It's Time to Talk about Feelings," *Time*, http://time.com/3774596/american-teens-emotions/ (April 10, 2015).
6. Neil Postman, *Amusing Ourselves to Death: Public Discourse in the Age of Show Business (New York, NY:* Viking Press, 1985) Page xix.AGE?

CHAPTER 23

1. Ephesians 4:11–12.

CHAPTER 24

1. Carrie Baron, M.D., "Creativity, Happiness, and Your Own Two Hands," *Psychology Today*, https://www.psychologytoday.com/us/blog/the-creativity-cure/201205/creativity-happiness-and-your-own-two-hands (May 3, 2012).

2. "Neuroscientist Says Working with Your Hands Is Good for Your Brain," Neurocore Brain Performace Centers, https://www .neurocorecenters.com/blog/neuroscientist-says-working-with-your -hands-is-good-for-your-brain (May 3, 2018).

CHAPTER 25

1. Julia Cameron, "The Road Less Travelled: Artist Date Suggestion," JuliaCameronLive, https://juliacameronlive.com/2012/01/04/33437/ (Jan. 4, 2012).
2. Sara Bernard, "Neuroplasticity: Learning Physically Challenges the Brain," Edutopia, https://www.edutopia.org/neuroscience-brain -based-learning-neuroplasticity (Dec. 1, 2010).
3. Jason Flom, "Talking Points: Your Brain on Learning," Cornerstone Learning Community, http://cornerstonelc.com/talking-points-your -brain-on-learning/ (April 23, 2012).

CHAPTER 26

1. Dan Hunter, "Imagination Precedes Creativity," Hunter-IQ.com, https://hunter-iq.com/imagination-precedes-creativity/ (July 6, 2017).
2. Reva Seth, "The Scientific Reasons Why Your To-Do List Is Bad for You," FastCompany.com, https://www.fastcompany.com/3054543/ the-scientific-reasons-why-your-to-do-list-is-bad-for-you (Dec. 14, 2015).
3. Aly Juma, "Da Vinci's To Do List: Inside the Mind of a Genius," Alyjuma.com, https://alyjuma.com/da-vincis-to-do/.

CHAPTER 27

1. Amy Ellis Nutt, "Why Kids and Teens May Face Far More Anxiety these Days," *Washington Post*, https://www.washingtonpost.com/news/ to-your-health/wp/2018/05/10/why-kids-and-teens-may-face-far -more-anxiety-these-days/?utm_term=.8a570adb2b2f (May 10, 2018).
2. Ibid.
3. "Any Anxiety Disorder," National Institute of Mental Health, https:// www.nimh.nih.gov/health/statistics/any-anxiety-disorder.shtml (updated November 2017).
4. Kim Painter, "Teens aren't grasping 'the responsibilities of adulthood,'

new study says," *USA Today*, https://www.usatoday.com/story/news/2017/09/19/teens-grow-up-slower-study/105758486/ (Sept. 19, 2017).

CHAPTER 28

1. "Declining Dopamine May Explain Why Older People Take Less Risks," Neuroscience News, https://neurosciencenews.com/aging-risk-dopamine-4359/ (June 2, 2016).
2. Matthew 6:34.

CONCLUSION

1. Romans 12:2.

New Video Study for Your Church or Small Group

If you've enjoyed this book, now you can go deeper with the companion video Bible study!

In this five-session study, Rebekah Lyons helps you apply the principles in *Rhythms of Renewal* to your life. The study guide includes video notes, group discussion questions, and personal study and reflection materials for in-between sessions.

Study Guide
9780310098850

DVD
9780310098874

Available now at your favorite bookstore,
or streaming video on StudyGateway.com.

You Are Free

Be Who You Already Are

Rebekah Lyons

You don't have to keep striving for freedom; live in the freedom you already have in Christ. In these pages, Rebekah Lyons walks you through her journey of releasing stress, anxiety, and worry to uncover the peace that is offered to us through Jesus Christ.

Have you bought the lie? Many of us do. We measure our worth by what others think of us. We compare and strive, existing mostly for the approval of others. Pressure rises, fear and anxiety creep in, and we hustle to keep up.

But Jesus whispers, I gave my life to set you free. I gave you purpose. I called you to live in freedom in that purpose. Yet we still hobble through life, afraid to confess all the ways we push against this truth, because we can't even believe it.

Christ doesn't say you can be or may be or will be free. He says you are free. Dare you believe it?

In *You Are Free*, Rebekah invites you to:

- Overcome the exhaustion of trying to meet the expectations of others and rest in the joy God's freedom brings.
- Find permission to grieve past experiences, confess areas of brokenness, and receive strength in your journey toward healing.
- Throw off self-condemnation, burn superficial masks, and step boldly into what our good God has for you.
- Discover the courage to begin again and use your newfound freedom to set others free.

Freedom is for everyone who wants it—the lost, the wounded, and those weary from all of the striving. It's for those who gave up trying years ago. It's for those angry and hurt, brilliant and burnt by the Christian song and dance. You are the church, the people of God. You were meant to be free.

Available in stores and online!